Chapters in a Life
of Paul

Chapters in a Life of Paul

John Knox

Revised by the author and
edited and introduced by
Douglas R. A. Hare

SCM PRESS LTD

226.9

334 01918 4

First publshed 1950
This revised edition first published in Britain 1989
by SCM Press Ltd
26–30 Tottenham Road, London N1 4BZ

Typeset in the United States of America
and printed in Great Britain by
The Camelot Press Ltd
Southampton

Contents

Part 3
The Man in Christ

Preface
to the Revised Edition

This book is concerned with the life of Paul as distinguished from his thought, but it is not a "life of Paul." Rather it is an attempt to deal with a few of the problems a writer of such a life would have to consider, either as preliminary to, or in the course of, his work. Although some of the questions it treats are of the greatest importance to the study of Paul's life, I would not for a moment claim that all of them together are the most important questions that could be asked. A number of the most basic and difficult problems are hardly mentioned—for example, the historical and sociological background of Paul's career. The questions are those, important and less important, on which I have ventured to hope I might have something useful to say.

The basic hypothesis concerning the chronology of Paul's career, defended in chapters 3-5 of this book, was originally presented in two articles of mine: " 'Fourteen Years Later'—A Note on the Pauline Chronology," *Journal of Religion* 16 (1936): 341-49, and "The Pauline Chronology," *Journal of Biblical Literature* 58 (1939): 15-29. A book that sought to elaborate, refine, and further defend this hypothesis was published in 1950 by Abingdon Press. The present work represents a revision of that book.

In this revision I have made free use of my essay in *Colloquy on New Testament Studies*, ed. Bruce C. Corley (Macon GA: Mercer University Press, 1983) 339-64. I thank that Press for permission to do so.

Both the publishers and I joined in asking Professor Douglas R. A. Hare to serve as editor of this edition. In that capacity, he has given me indispensable editorial counsel and help, besides taking responsibility for writing the introduction, preparing the typescript for publication, and seeing the book through the press. Without his assistance it could not have been published. I am very grateful.

John Knox

Introduction

A full half-century has elapsed since John Knox published his first seminal article on the chronology of Paul's career. Its opening words challenged the learned readers of the *Journal of Religion* to adopt a more adequate historical method for dealing with this vexed subject.

It does not need to be said that our principal sources for the life of Paul are the letters generally esteemed authentic and the several sections of Luke-Acts that deal with his career. It is equally unnecessary to add that of these the letters are by all odds the more important and in cases of conflict with Acts, whether explicit or implied, are always to be followed. This is probably obvious enough and yet is often ignored.[1]

The article proceeded to sketch out in broad strokes what a chronology of Paul would look like if one were to depend almost entirely on the epistles. A sequel published three years later further amplified the proposal. The methodological idea was clear enough, and it was adopted readily by one of Knox's teachers, Donald W. Riddle, for his book *Paul, Man of Conflict*.[2] It was not until 1950, however, that Knox issued the fuller treatment of his proposal represented by *Chapters in a Life of Paul*.

Originally prepared for oral delivery as the Quillian Lectures at Emory University, *Chapters* is a model of lucidity and is little cumbered by the scholarly footnotes that normally adorn significant contributions to such

---

[1]John Knox, " 'Fourteen Years Later': A Note on the Pauline Chronology," *Journal of Religion* 16 (1936): 341.

[2]John Knox, "The Pauline Chronology," *Journal of Biblical Literature* 58 (1939): 15-29; D. W. Riddle, *Paul, Man of Conflict* (New York and Nashville: Abingdon-Cokesbury, 1940).

discussions. Those not yet initiated into the mysteries of higher criticism can read the book with little difficulty (a few Greek words do appear, and technical terms are used occasionally), but this must not mislead us into regarding it as a work of little account. It is one of the most important studies of Paul to appear in our century.

This volume was bound to be controversial because it insisted that there is only one way to produce a dependable reconstruction of Paul's career. Whereas others felt obliged to treat the account of that career in the Book of Acts as largely accurate, to be supplemented and perhaps at points corrected by autobiographical allusions in Paul's letters, Knox propounded the thesis that proper historical method requires us to draw a *sharp* distinction between the primary source consisting of the epistles and this secondary source of later date and uncertain origin. While acknowledged in principle by most serious scholars, this distinction becomes blurred beyond recognition in the work of many. The consequence is a plethora of attempted harmonizations of the two sources. John Knox cut the Gordian knot by rigorously subordinating the secondary to the primary source: " . . . a fact only suggested in the letters has a status which even the most unequivocal statement of Acts, it not otherwise supported, cannot confer."[3] Focusing in this way on the data provided by the letters alone, Knox was able to produce an outline of Paul's career that was coherent, faithful to the apostle's own testimony, and disengaged from the various problems (such as fourteen to seventeen "silent years") that so plagued the harmonizing reconstructions.

While a small number of scholars were delighted with this approach and its results, it is not surprising that many more reacted negatively. One of the early reviewers, George Ogg, while praising "the excellent exposition of the phrase 'in Christ' " in the latter part of *Chapters,* found Knox's treatment of Acts well nigh irresponsible (although he stopped just short of saying this).[4] Ogg correctly perceived the importance to Knox's outline of Gal. 2:10: "Only they would have us remember the poor, which very thing I was eager to do." According to Knox this text refers not to a request that Paul's Gentile converts give regularly to the poor in their respective communities or send charitable donations continually to Jerusalem

---

[3]See below, 19.

[4]George Ogg, "A New Chronology of Saint Paul's Life," *Expository Times* 64 (1952-1953): 120-23.

but rather to a specific, one time project, the great collection, about which
Paul speaks at length in 1 Cor. 16:1-4, 2 Cor. 8-9 and Rom. 15:25-31. (For
the argument, see below, pp. 37-40.) Ogg was unimpressed; "To do that
was with him a heartfelt desire, and he may well have been every whit as
much concerned about a collection for the poor several years after the Jerusalem Conference as he can have been immediately after it was over."[5]
The point is critical. It is lamentable that the reviewer did not feel the need
to support his critique of Knox at this point with more than a weak conjecture concerning Paul's charitable impulses. Knox's case is carefully argued on the basis of numerous details in the texts, and deserves a fuller
response from any who choose to oppose it. One cannot help feeling that
Ogg, like others in his train, was uninterested in the specifics of the argument in the way a scientist is uninterested in the details of a presentation
he regards as pseudoscientific; Knox had disqualified himself from serious
consideration by his dismissal of Acts as a reliable historical source.

Another British scholar, George Caird, was even more forthright on
this issue: "This theory naturally avoids all the difficulties which beset those
who take Acts more seriously. . . . "[6] He mistakenly infers that Knox's
decision to ignore the Acts framework is based on an *assumption*—"the
assumption that it was not drawn from Luke's sources but was his own editorial contribution. . . . "[7] Knox's treatment of Acts is by no means so
cavalier or prejudicial. After carefully considering statements in Luke's
account that are clearly contradicted by Paul's own testimony, Knox properly asks: if Luke's chronological accuracy can be proved deficient where
a parallel source permits comparison, what justification do we have for
trusting him implicitly where no parallel is extant? In defense of Knox
against the charge of not taking Acts seriously, it must be said that the author of *Chapters* does indeed take Acts with utmost seriousness; instead of
assuming its reliability he subjects it to the rigorous cross-examination that
is required in good historiography. He finds the second half of Acts (beginning at 15:41; cf. Gal. 1:21) much more dependable and concludes that,
whereas Luke had more consecutive sources (including perhaps primarily

---

[5]Ibid., 122.

[6]George Caird, "Chronology of the New Testament," *Interpreter's Dictionary
of the Bible* (New York and Nashville: Abingdon, 1952) 1:606.

[7]Ibid.

the so-called "We"-source) for these later chapters, he had only fragmentary accounts for the earlier period and was thus compelled to piece them together as well as he could. If Luke moved the Jerusalem Conference to an earlier position in Paul's career and separated it from the great collection, which was intended both by Paul and by the leaders of the Jerusalem church as a "peace offering," it was because Luke was eager to show that the Judaizing controversy, far from seriously threatening the concord of the church, was settled early and definitively.

Another early response to the Knox chronology was made by Thomas Campbell, who followed Knox's method in part, in an attempt to demonstrate the reliability of Acts. Drawing on statements in the epistles, Campbell showed that Paul's missionary itinerary could be established as Syria, Cilicia, Macedonia, Achaia, and Asia. This series corresponds strikingly with the sequence reported by Acts. The epistles give no clear indication of where Galatia fits in the series, but it is legitimate to accept the testimony of Acts: "If Acts gives a reliable report of the progress of Paul's missionary work in Macedonia, Achaia and Asia, are we not justified in assuming that it may give us an equally reliable report of his work in Galatia?"[8]

This may, indeed, be a legitimate inference, but we must be careful regarding the conclusions we draw from Campbell's brief study. W. G. Kümmel, for example, cites the Campbell article as demonstrating "that we have good grounds for deriving the relative chronology of Paul's activity from a critical combination of the information from Paul's letters with the account in Acts," and he then proceeds to place *all* the missionary activity in Asia Minor and Greece *after* the Jerusalem Conference, apparently because he regards as reliable Luke's location of Paul's second visit to Jerusalem (Gal. 2:1-10) as early as Acts 11:30.[9] Campbell's study, however, does not demonstrate the reliability of the earlier chapters of Acts. Indeed, Campbell concedes that there is apparently some confusion in Acts concerning this second visit: "The more elaborate account in Acts 15, which included the account of the 'decrees,' may be a doublet."[10] But to

---

[8]T. H. Campbell, "Paul's 'Missionary Journeys' as Reflected in His Letters," *Journal of Biblical Literature* 74 (1955): 87.

[9]W. G. Kümmel, *Introduction to the New Testament,* trans. H. C. Kee (New York and Nashville: Abingdon, 1975) 254.

[10]Ibid., 255.

admit this, as Kümmel also seems to do, is to acknowledge that Acts may also not be entirely reliable on the *location* of the visit. If Luke's sources provided him with two different accounts of this visit, which he was able to place at different points in his story, it is probable that one or both of these sources contained little indication of the timing of the conference relative to Paul's missionary work.

What Campbell and Kümmel seem to overlook is that *Chapters* said no less than Campbell's article regarding Acts' testimony concerning the sequence of missionary stations.

> We have good reason to trust the Acts account of the general order in which this work was done. According to that account he went first to Galatia, then to Macedonia, down the Greek peninsula, and finally to Ephesus and Asia. The letters nowhere contradict, and often confirm, this story. Since Galatia is the easternmost of the provinces mentioned, it is to be assumed that he would work there first.[11]

What distinguishes Knox from his critics is that he refuses to be misled by the evidence of correlation between the epistles and Acts on this sequence into a less critical approach to Luke's presentation of Paul's relationship with Jerusalem. Since Luke is clearly mistaken concerning the nature of the first visit (Acts 9:26-30; cf. Gal. 1:18-20) and is confused about the second (Acts 11:30, 15:1-30, cf. Gal. 2:1-10), what right do we have to any assurance that he correctly places this conference before Paul's activity in Macedonia, Achaia and Asia?[12]

Further support for the proposal that the conference visit has been misplaced by Acts was provided by an article by Donald Rowlingson, "The Jerusalem Conference and Jesus' Nazareth Visit: A Study in Pauline Chronology." A comparison of the Third Gospel with Mark and Matthew suggests that its author was not averse to moving an important incident to an earlier point in the structure of his narrative in order to display more fully its theological significance. Rowlingson concludes,

---

[11]John Knox, *Chapters in a Life of Paul,* 1st ed. (New York and Nashville: Abingdon-Cokesbury, 1950) 79.

[12]A telling critique of Campbell's article is presented by J. C. Hurd, "Pauline Chronology and Pauline Theology," *Christian History and interpretation: Studies Presented to John Knox,* ed. W. R. Farmer, C. F. D. Moule, and R. R. Niebuhr (Cambridge: University Press, 1967) 228-31.

Although the parallel is not exact, the Jerusalem Conference does reassert at a strategic point certain of the major interests of Acts which have been set forth decisively in its overture (1:1-11, especially vv. 6-8). Its position is such as to anticipate the major conquest of the Gentile world which takes place during Paul's labors around the Aegean Sea, even though prior to this time indications of that conquest have already been given.[13]

Another early supporter was Jack Suggs. In his article "Concerning the Date of Paul's Macedonian Ministry," Suggs defended Knox's proposal that Philippians 4:15 (" . . . in the beginning of the gospel, when I left Macedonia . . . ") suggests a relatively early date for Paul's arrival in Europe. Knox was right, he urged, in maintaining that the allusion to Syria and Cilicia in Gal. 1:21 does not exclude subsequent missionary work further west prior to the second visit to Jerusalem; indeed it is not even clear that these two areas are mentioned here by Paul as *mission fields:* "Gal. 1:21 mentions Syria and Cilicia for the same reason that 1:17 mentions Arabia and Damascus—namely to show Paul's independence of Jerusalem. The passage proves nothing as to whether any one or all four of these places were fields of the apostle's missionary activity."[14] Suggs observes that Syria and Cilicia may not have been regarded by Paul as the kind of "virgin territory" constituting his special responsibility (cf. Rom. 15:20).[15]

No attempt can be made in this brief introduction to list all the scholars who supported, opposed or ignored the Knox proposal. The earlier history of this debate has been helpfully documented by John Hurd in the Knox *Festschrift.*[16] Here, as in his earlier work *The Origin of 1 Corinthians,* Hurd shows himself a strong supporter of Knox's method and suggests that further supporting evidence can be obtained by setting the epistles in sequence on the basis of Paul's treatment of various theological motifs.[17]

A new phase in the debate was inititated in 1979-1980 with the publication of two books devoted specifically to the problem of Pauline chro-

---

[13]Donald Rowlingson, "The Jerusalem Conference and Jesus' Nazareth visit: A study in Pauline Chronology," *Journal of Biblical Literature* 71 (1952): 71.

[14]Jack Suggs, "Concerning the Date of Paul's Macedonian Ministry," *Novum Testamentum* 4 (1960): 67.

[15]Ibid.

[16]See note 12 above.

[17]See John Hurd, *The Origin of 1 Corinthians* (London: S.P.C.K., 1965) 12-42.

nology as articulated by John Knox. The first of these, in terms of
publication date, Robert Jewett's *A Chronology of Paul's Life*, strongly
concurred with Knox that the Jerusalem Conference should be placed late
in Paul's career at a point corresponding roughly to the fourth visit reported by Luke (18:22).[18] Jewett insisted, however, that the data of Acts
be treated less skeptically than it was treated by Knox. Wherever we can
detect no evidence of redactional manipulation and we can suppose that
Luke is using sources, there is no reason why we should not ascribe to the
chronological details an "experimental" value.[19] Details provided by the
letters are clearly of superior worth, and there is no justification for the
harmonizations that attribute equal value to Luke's schedule of five visits.
"A general rule therefore is that material from Acts is usable in the chronological experiment only when it does not conflict with evidence in the letters."[20] As Hurd points out, however, this marks a significant departure
from the Knox method. If conflict can be demonstrated where the letters
provide relevant evidence, how can we be confident of using chronological details from Acts where such testing is not possible?[21] An instance that
might be cited is Jewett's dependence on the Acts context of 18:22 for lo-
cating Paul's private conference with the Jerusalem leaders; he seems to
accept without cross-examination Luke's confused testimony regarding
Paul's activity in Ephesus prior to his departure for Jerusalem.[22] There is
nothing in 1 Corinthians to suggest that this second visit was prompted by
experiences with Judaizers in Corinth, and consequently it is improbable
that Paul set off for Jerusalem after spending only a weekend in Ephesus
(Acts 18:19-21). Even if Luke is in possession of a dependable source for

---

[18]Robert Jewett, *A Chronology of Paul's Life* (Philadelphia: Fortress, 1979)
78, 89-93.

[19]Ibid., 22.

[20]Ibid., 24.

[21]Hurd complains that Jewett "uses Acts as a major source and is willing to
confirm items in it by other material from the same source. He is even willing . . .
to allow the cumulative weight of details from Acts to outweigh data from the letters." John Hurd, "Seminar on Pauline Chronology: Introduction," *Colloquy on
New Testament Studies*, ed. Bruce Corley (Macon GA: Mercer University Press,
1983) 267.

[22]Jewett, *Chronology*, 97-98.

Paul's itinerary on this trip, we cannot infer therefrom that he is well informed concerning its precise timing and motivation.

Written prior to Jewett's book but published a year later, Gerd Luedemann's *Paulus, der Heidenapostel*, vol. 1: *Studien zur Chronologie* (Göttingen, 1980) is available in English as *Paul, Apostle to the Gentiles: Studies in Chronology* (Fortress, 1984). Luedemann rigorously follows the method proposed by Knox. In his first chapter he devotes careful attention to the question of Luke's accuracy regarding data drawn from secular history, and makes important observations on the way this author assembled his traditions. Seldom noticed, for example, is the way Luke groups reports concerning incidents involving Paul in Philippi and Corinth, for example, in his first visits to these cities, reporting nothing of substance for subsequent visits. It seems likely, as Luedemann urges, that this bunching of incidents represents redaction rather than history. Thus, even if we were to accept as reliable Luke's story about Jews haling Paul before Gallio (Luedemann gives sound reasons for caution), we should nonetheless ask whether Luke was well informed, or careful in reporting, the precise location of this incident; it may just as well have occurred during another visit to Corinth.[23]

In his second chapter Luedemann proceeds to reconstruct a chronology of Paul's career based entirely on the letters. He builds upon Knox's treatment of Gal. 2:10 as referring to the great collection, but argues that Knox allowed too short a time between the conference and offering visits; at least three and more probably four years must be postulated to accommodate the activities of this period. Knox recognized the force of this argument and has adopted Luedemann's "three or four years" in this revised edition of *Chapters*. There are differences of detail between Luedemann and Knox. For example, Luedemann proposes that the congregations addressed in Galatians were located in the northern part of the province and were founded *after* the church in Corinth during an illness Paul suffered while en route from Corinth to Antioch.[24] He locates the dispute with Peter at Antioch (Gal. 2:11-14) *prior* to the Jerusalem Conference of Gal. 2:1-10.[25]

Luedemann's third chapter is devoted to a study of some of the Pauline traditions in Acts. He concludes that it is "likely that Luke used a list of

---

[23]Cf. Luedemann, *Paul*, 17-18.

[24]Ibid., 108.

[25]Ibid., 75-77.

stations embellished with various episodes and that this source derived from
a companion of Paul,'' and that it undergirds Acts 16-20. Traditions such
as those alluding to the expulsion of Priscilla and Aquila from Rome and
the conversion of Crispus can be regarded as reliable ''once they have been
integrated into the framework obtained solely on the basis of the letters''
and thus ''attain to a historical value almost equal to that of the primary
source.''[26]

The publication of the volumes by Jewett and Luedemann in close
succession prompted a renewed interest in the book on which they both,
in different ways, depended, namely *Chapters in a Life of Paul*. The or-
ganizers of the Colloquy on New Testament Studies, ''A Time for Reap-
praisal and Fresh Approaches,'' held in 1980 at Southwestern Baptist
Theological Seminary, convened a seminar devoted specifically to Pauline
chronology. Moderated by John Hurd, the seminar featured papers presented personally by Jewett and Luedemann. The subsequent discussion
involving the moderator, the two authors and learned participants is helpfully documented in *Colloquy on New Testament Studies*, edited by Bruce
Corley.[27] To the seminar papers and discussion report has been added an
important article by John Knox, ''Chapters in a Life of Paul—A Response
to Robert Jewett and Gerd Luedemann.''

In this essay, written thirty years after his book was published, Knox
reaffirms in the strongest terms his basic methodological principle.

> The incomparable value of the letters . . . is such (a) that the merest hint
> in the letters is to be deemed worth more than the most explicit statement
> in Acts; (b) that a statement in Acts about Paul is to be regarded as incred-
> ible if it conflicts directly with the letters (as many statements do) and is
> to be seriously questioned even if a conflict is only suggested; and (c) that
> statements about Paul in Acts are to be accepted with confidence only if
> such statements are fully and explicitly confirmed by the letters. . . . There
> can be no doubt that [Acts] contains true traditions of facts and episodes
> in Paul's life, but these traditions can never have the certitude which data
> obtained from the letters possess.[28]

---

[26]Ibid., 156, 177. Jewett suggests that Luedemann is insufficiently cautious in
this respect (*Colloquy*, 283).

[27]See note 21 above.

[28]*Colloquy*, 342.

For strict adherence to this principle Luedemann receives high praise from Knox; his work is hailed "as the most impressive exposition and defense so far of a chronology based entirely on the letters."[29] He implicitly questions Luedemann's confidence in Acts at certain points, however, as for example in his observation, "There is really no evidence in the letters that Paul and Barnabas ever worked together . . . only in Acts are the two represented as being actual collaborators. . . . "[30] In more emphatic language than in his 1950 volume, Knox rejects the notion of the "first missionary journey" as reported in Acts 13-14: such a journey did not occur as part of Paul's career.[31]

Respecting Jewett's work, Knox professes perplexity. Despite Jewett's explicit acknowledgment of adherence to Knox's basic outline, his methodology differs greatly from that proposed in *Chapters*. In response to Jewett's protestation, "No single detail from Acts, it seems to me, deserves to be raised to the level of independent credibility," Knox queries, "But is this principle consistently applied? As I read Jewett's book, I do not get the impression that it is. . . . He follows Acts, provided Paul's letters do not clearly preclude his doing so, the notable exception being his association of the conference with Acts 18 rather than 15. This method accounts for what I regard as flaws in his chronology itself."[32]

This stimulating debate provides reason enough for reprinting *Chapters*. It must be noted, however, that this revised edition is not simply a reprint. Significant additions, deletions and alterations have been made by the author, especially in chapter 5. Originally entitled "Places and Dates," the revised chapter bears the title "A Biographical Sketch." In it Knox has incorporated a good deal of material from his essay in *Colloquy*, since it well represents the modifications of his original outline which years of reflection and the current debate have suggested. It should be observed that he now regards it as virtually certain that the intervals mentioned by Paul in Gal. 1-2 ("after three years," "after fourteen years") are nonconcurrent, that is, that the second visit takes place seventeen years after Paul's conversion, not fourteen as he had allowed for as not improbable in the

---

[29]Ibid., 359.

[30]Ibid., 361.

[31]See below, 58-59.

[32]Jewett, *Colloquy,* 281; Knox, ibid., 363.

first edition.[33] He also adopts Luedemann's proposal that the interval between the second and third Jerusalem visits must be at least three years and
possibly as much as four. Knox now consistently uses A.D. 34 for the date
of Paul's conversion (A.D. 35 appears on a number of occasions in the earlier edition). In place of the 1950 statement quoted above (p. xiii), "We
have good reason to trust the Acts account of the general order in which
this work was done," Knox now more cautiously proposes:

> What happened after his brief stay in Cilicia? I believe that *if we had
> only the letters as sources* (and we are here assuming for the moment that
> such were the case), the consensus of scholarly opinion would be that his
> course continued in a westerly direction and, since he can speak later of
> his preaching in Macedonia as being "in the beginning of the gospel" (Phil.
> 4:15), that after no long period he reached that province. . . . As to his
> route from Cilicia to Macedonia or as to events on the way, the letters alone
> would give us no clue. But his most direct route would have been through
> or near the cities of Iconium, Derbe, Lystra, Antioch, and perhaps other
> places in southern Galatia. . . . Acts 15:41-16:12 tells us that Paul reached
> Macedonia by way of Syria and Cilicia and the cities of southern Galatia,
> and it may not be irrelevant in this connection to observe that it is toward
> the end of this account of Paul's journey from Cilicia to Philippi that the
> so-called "diary" makes its first appearance.[34]

What is perhaps most distinctive of Knox's most recent treatment of
the mission in Galatia is his categorical denial to Barnabas of any part in
it. The letter to the Galatians, he notes, stresses unambiguously that it was
Paul and no other who first brought the gospel to the addressees: "The letter, throughout and in the most emphatic way, identifies them as *his*
churches. *He* founded them; *he* has nurtured them; *he* has made two visits
to them (4:13)."[35] The possibility of a late date for Galatians, proposed by
his student Howard Ramsey in a Columbia University dissertation and
adopted by Knox in his article on Galatians in the *Interpreter's Dictionary
of the Bible*, is favored in the revised edition over a date during the Ephesian period as suggested in the first edition.[36]

---

[33]*Chapters*, 1st ed., 77-78, 83.

[34]See below, 57.

[35]*Colloquy*, 349; see below, 60.

[36]H. L. Ramsey, "The Place of Galatians in the Career of Paul" (Ph.D. diss.,
Columbia University, 1960); John Knox, "Galatians, Letter to the," *Interpreter's Dictionary of the Bible*, 2:338-43. See below, 62.

Up to this point we have been concerned almost exclusively with the earlier segments of *Chapters*, those dealing with matters of chronology. It is not surprising that John Knox has expressed disappointment that the later chapters, those concerning "The Man and His Work" and "The Man in Christ," have received so little attention in scholarly discussion. Particularly treasured by him for this reason is a handwritten note of appreciation from Henry J. Cadbury of Harvard, praising his book for its "admirable analysis of Paul's human personality which is a topic in which books are strangely lacking" and its "courageous and highly successful attempt to put down his religion in the balance and articulation which is so much truer to Paul than most Pauline theologies."[37] Cadbury's evaluation is fully justified. Knox's later chapters can by no means be regarded as offering an outline of Paul's theology; such was not the author's intent. They do, however, provide a vivid sketch of the personality of Paul and of the core of his religious experience. Paul's life and thought were molded by the revelation to him of the resurrected Christ. He was able to "recognize" this heavenly personage because of what Knox calls his "previous knowledge of Christ," drawn not from a personal glimpse of the Nazarene in Jerusalem but from the church's "living memory of Jesus."[38] Because of the communal nature of this memory of Christ, who is simultaneously experienced in the church as alive through the Holy Spirit, the phrase "in Christ" is Paul's preferred way of alluding to the corporate dimension of the Christian's experience. In this connection Knox introduces concepts employed by him in his books on Jesus and the church: the Christ event and the new humanity. For Knox the Christ event includes the church as its empirical outcome.

> Jesus, then, is not simply the person; he is the representative and embodiment of a new kind of humanity, a humanity free from sin and from all threat of corruption and death. He, like Adam, represents an entire order of creation; he is the "second man." To know the risen Christ is to be made a participant in a whole new realm of the Spirit. To belong to Christ is to belong to a new, redeemed humanity.[39]

------

[37] Dr. Knox graciously lent me the letter, which is dated only "24 March." From its content I gather it was written soon after the book appeared in 1950.

[38] See below, 104.

[39] See below, 112.

Of particular interest is Knox's treatment of forgiveness and repen
tance in Paul's religious experience. The almost complete absence of the
pertinent terms from Paul's letters is especially astonishing in view of their
importance not only in the Scriptures and contemporary Judaism but in Jesus' teaching. Knox correctly insists that "the *substance* of repentance and
forgiveness is surely here" in Paul's Christian experience, but the traditional terms have been replaced by "justification" and "reconciliation,"
corresponding respectively to the justice and mercy of God. Knox laments
Paul's dissection of divine forgiveness into these two components as "one
of the most tragically fateful developments in the whole history of Christian theology."[40]

> But Paul by dividing forgiveness into two parts opened the way to division
> in the nature of God himself; his justice is seen as mere justice and his mercy
> as only mercy. He is the just Judge and the merciful Father; he is not, as
> he is for Jesus, a Father who is both just and merciful—truly (that is, ap-
> propriately) just only because he is also merciful, truly (that is, authenti-
> cally) merciful only because he is also just.[41]

Knox traces two regrettable results of this dichotomizing of the divine forgiveness: (1) the interpretation of Christ's death as a satisfaction of God's
righteous demands (which Knox regards as one of the least adequate of the
various "explanations" of the death of Jesus offered in the New Testament)
and (2) the loss of "the only possible theoretical ground for affirming the reality of ethical obligation within the Christian life."[42] The author is especially
troubled by this second problem, the theoretical antinomianism of Paul's
thought; he insists that Paul nowhere convincingly answers his opponents'
question: "Why then not sin that grace may abound?" (cf. Rom. 6:1).[43]

---

[40]See below, 120, 122.

[41]See below, 122.

[42]See below, 125-26.

[43]Knox further developed this thesis in *The Ethic of Jesus in the Teaching of
the Church* (New York and Nashville: Abingdon, 1961). Appreciative but critical
responses are provided by Paul Schubert, "Paul and the New Testament Ethic in
the Thought of John Knox," and C. F. D. Moule, "Obligation in the Ethic of
Paul," in *Christian History and Interpretation*, 363-88 and 389-406.

Chapters in a Life of Paul deserved to be reprinted even in unchanged form; the revisions introduced by the author make the republication all the more desirable. Despite the newer and fuller treatments by Jewett and Luedemann, the Knox volume is still the most useful teaching tool I know for presenting the problem of the relationship between the epistles and Acts to ordinary college students, seminarians, pastors, and adult church school classes. Even those who are inclined to disagree with Knox's conclusions will benefit greatly from the clarity with which he presents the problem and its attendant issues. As a teacher I am grateful indeed to Mercer University Press for making this important tool available again. And I have only the highest praise for John Knox, now in his eighty-sixth year, who with enthusiasm, speed and careful attention to detail prepared the revisions for this edition.

I would like finally to express my appreciation to Dean Ulrich Mauser of Pittsburgh Theological Seminary, who encouraged this project and made available the skilled secretarial services of Mrs. Joyce Thompson, assisted in part by Ms. Debora Hutchison, to both of whom my sincere thanks are also gratefully tendered.

Douglas R. A. Hare
William F. Orr Professor of New
Testament
Pittsburgh Theological Seminary
1 September 1986

Part 1

□

Concerning Sources

Chapter I

□────────────────────────────────□

The Nature of our Sources

It is commonly said that the student of the life of Paul faces a simpler problem, so far as sources are concerned, than does the student of the life of Jesus. At first sight, at least, such an observation seems unquestionably, even obviously, true. The difficulties involved in reconstructing the life of Jesus are enormous. We must depend almost entirely upon the four Gospels, the earliest of which was written a generation after the end of Jesus' career. Jesus himself wrote nothing; nor, so far as we know, did any of his disciples; and the memories of his words and of the incidents of his career were undoubtedly modified, probably sometimes beyond all recognition, during the long period when they circulated only in oral form. Such modification would be bound to occur in any case—stories always change as they are told and retold—but it was all the more likely in this case because of the developing Christian faith in the supreme significance of Jesus and of all that happened in connection with him. Memory was transfigured by faith. Not only would we suspect in advance that this would occur, but it can also easily be demonstrated that it did in fact take place.

Even after the first Gospel had been written, this process of change continued. The four Gospels differ widely and in quite remarkable ways from one another. This is true even of the three so-called Synoptic Gospels, which have a common literary basis; it becomes much more impressively true when we also take the Fourth Gospel into consideration. Indeed, if it should be decided that the Synoptic Gospels are as far from the original facts as the Fourth Gospel manifestly is from the Synoptics, we should have to resign ourselves to knowing virtually nothing at all about the historical Jesus or his life. As a matter of fact, however, although the tradition was involved in a process of change from the very beginning, that process was constantly accelerating and gathering momentum, so that we are not justified in distrusting the historical accuracy of the Synoptic Gospels to the extent that we are forced to doubt the historical accuracy of the Fourth Gospel. Still, in Mark no less certainly, even if less extensively, than in John "history" is shot through with "interpretation," and the careful historian must strive to allow for this fact. It is because there are so many points where we are unable to make this allowance with any assurance that the task of writing a life of Jesus is so enormously difficult.

In comparison, the writing of a life of Paul would at first appear to be a much simpler undertaking. We now have a firsthand source—some letters from the apostle's own hand. We possess also, in the Acts of the Apostles, a straightforward narrative of his life, from the time when he was still a persecutor of the new faith until his arrival in Rome at the very end of his career, with occasional references to his earlier life. It is true that the letters, rich though they are as sources for the ideas, the personality, and the religious experience of the apostle, have little to tell us about his life. But the book of Acts, it is usually held, satisfactorily makes up for the autobiographical omissions of the letters. Thus emerges the usual picture of Paul's career: a Jew with the Jewish name of Saul, born in Tarsus in Cilicia, educated in Jerusalem at the feet of Gamaliel, a persecutor of the church in Judea, converted to Christianity on the "road to Damascus," making three great missionary journeys which took him from Antioch in Syria to regions as far west as Macedonia and Greece, finally arrested on a visit to Jerusalem, appealing to Caesar after several hearings before local magistrates, arriving at last in Rome for his trial and presumably his execution. How simple and clear, as compared with the vague and often contradictory materials available for the biography of Jesus!

But have we the right to this assurance? Must we not recognize that this appearance of greater simplicity and clarity is, at least in large part, deceptive? Imagine for a moment that instead of having four Gospels we had only one—say, the Gospel of Luke. It is obvious that then our picture of the career of Jesus would be simpler and clearer than it is. But is it not equally obvious that this greater simplicity and clarity would be specious and false? A clear and simple account is of no value if it is not also a true account. Partly because we can compare Luke with Matthew, and especially with Mark, we are in a position to know that this evangelist's account cannot be accepted as a true and simple narrative of facts in their original order and with their original meaning. If we did not have Matthew and Mark, we might not know this—certainly not as well. But Luke's account would not be any truer because of our ignorance. The analogy with Acts is not exact, of course; but if we had three other records of Paul's career, written, say, between A.D. 90 and 130, our conception of the movement of that career would undoubtedly be far less clear and definite than it is—and far less mistaken. Why should we suppose that Luke, who can be shown to have had meager sources and to have made independent, although admittedly careful and responsible, use of those he had when he wrote the first volume of his work, had adequate sources and simply recorded what they clearly told him when he wrote his second volume? This fortuitous absence of parallel accounts does not justify us in being less critical of Acts than we are forced to be of Luke.

Fortunately, however, we are not altogether without a "parallel account." This is to be found in the letters, which provide us with more of a check on Acts, even as regards the external, chronological course of Paul's career, than has been usually supposed.

But we are getting too far ahead of our story! Ground must be laid in the form of some considerations of a more general kind about these two sources for the life of Paul.

I

We may appropriately begin by noting that, like the Gospels, the documents on which we must depend for our knowledge of Paul came into being in their present form for the use of the Gentile churches of the late first and early second centuries and in response to their interests and needs; and that, again as in the case of the Gospels, we can gain trustworthy knowledge of the original facts only by allowing accurately for the effect of the later situation on the documentary sources. Let us examine this fact as it relates first to the letters and then to the Acts of the Apostles.

We have already observed as a major difference between the sources for Jesus and for Paul the fact that Paul left behind writings from his own hand whereas Jesus did not. This difference is obviously of the greatest importance. Spoken words circulating within a community over a period of time are more susceptible to various social pressures and are more likely to be modified by the practical uses to which they are put than words committed to writing. To be sure, one may easily press this principle too far: a few minutes with a harmony of the Gospels, for example, will reveal that often even after a saying of Jesus had been put into written form, as in Mark or Q, Matthew or Luke did not refrain from altering it; and on the other hand, the most characteristic teachings of Jesus, even though put into writing only a generation afterward, bear marks of authenticity as convincing as do any of Paul's letters. Still, the fact that Paul wrote letters, some of them quite long as letters go, gives the student of his life a decided advantage. Granting the fullest measure of authenticity to the teachings of Jesus in the Synoptic Gospels, we have only scattered sayings of the Master, not connected discourses, whereas for Paul we have massive consecutive utterances. And yet, as far as the formal fact is concerned, the same thing can be said of Paul's writings as of Jesus' sayings: they did not achieve the form in which they have survived until a generation or so after their author's death. This happened only when someone collected and edited his letters—just as another had earlier collected and edited the words of Jesus[1]—and, as has been said, this collecting and editing took place in response to the needs, and for the use, of the churches of the late first and early second centuries.

We do not know the name of the collector and editor—if indeed a single individual was responsible[2]—and we cannot know just what his motives were. We should expect, however, that such a one would be moved principally by devotion to Paul and by the conviction that what Paul had written to several churches between A.D. 40 and 60 was important to the entire church of a generation later. Possibly the collector was concerned

---

[1]The reader must not be confused by this individualizing of the collector and editor in each case, for the reference is not necessarily to a single person. Our Gospels represent the culmination of a long and gradual process. Although in my judgment an individual or a small group was responsible for the original collection of Paul's letters, we cannot rule out the possibility that, as some scholars believe, there were several distinct stages in this development as in the case of the Gospels. Nothing of importance for the present subject depends upon one's view of this matter.

[2]The fact that a personal letter was included in this collection of letters to the churches, as well as several other features, might be explained, as I have ventured to suggest in my *Philemon Among the Letters of Paul* (Chicago: University of Chicago Press, 1935; rev. ed., Nashville: Abingdon, 1959), if the collector was Onesimus or if the collection was made under his oversight as Bishop of Ephesus.

about the danger of Paul's being remembered and esteemed by only a small group of churches, of his becoming a mere party leader or symbol. Paul had been the center of no little controversy in his day; the original issues were dead, but perhaps the memory of old battles still hung about his name and kept him from being as widely known and appreciated as this disciple of his knew he deserved. But for whatever reason, he wanted to make Paul available and acceptable to the churches everywhere. References to Paul's letters, or unmistakable reminiscences of their language, in Christian writings from A.D. 95 onward, and from Syria across the world to Rome, bear witness to the success of his undertaking.

We can be sure the editor did not leave the letters just as he found them. Although we may not always be able to discern his hand—and the more skillful he was as an editor the less likely it is that we shall—his work has undoubtedly left its mark on the letter collection. We know that he gathered or perhaps selected the letters, that he arranged them in what he regarded as an appropriate order, that he determined their general format as the several parts of a single work. We know that he joined together materials from two or more letters to make what we know as 2 Corinthians; he may have done the same thing in the case of Philippians. It is often held that he placed a note to Ephesus at the end of the Epistle to the Romans, although why he should have done such a thing has never been persuasively explained. Many scholars have argued that he rewrote sections of Colossians, and it is more than possible that he did. He almost certainly made, as any editor would, many occasional interpolations, glosses, or omissions, with a view to clarifying, as he saw it, the meaning of the apostle. On the whole, however, he does not seem to have dealt drastically with the text of the letters, even when, as we may well believe, the apostle's polemic words scarcely suited his own irenic purpose. Such restraint on his part can be explained in several possible ways; by his own reverence for Paul, by the probability that the letters were severally too well known within local areas for large-scale revision to be feasible, or by the fact that no urgent need for radically reinterpreting Paul had yet arisen, such as developed later when heretical teachers were using his letters as their authorities. It is not unlikely that all three of these considerations have some relevance and force, but the really important explanation of the collector's restraint is the fact that he had chosen another way rather than textual revision or interpolation to bring Paul directly into touch with the problems and needs of his own period.

II

This other way was pseudepigraphy. Taking Colossians as his model, but using material from other letters also, the collector (or some predecessor or associate) wrote a fresh "letter of Paul"—this one addressed, not to one of the churches or a small group of them, as Paul's letters had been, but to "the saints who are also faithful in Christ Jesus." In it the divisive controversies of Paul's own period, that is, between the "apostle to the Gentiles" and the Judaizers, are relegated to the past, and the unity of the church is hailed as an accomplished fact.

> For he is our peace, who has made us both one, and has broken down the dividing wall of hostility, . . . that he might create in himself one new man in place of the two, so making peace, and might reconcile us both to God in one body through the cross, thereby bringing the hostility to an end. And he came and preached peace to you who were far off and peace to those who were near; for through him we both have access in one Spirit to the Father. (Eph. 2:14-18)

New sectarian tendencies, however, are already at work. Paul's doctrine, implicit in all of his letters, of the universality and oneness of the church is now, in his name, explicitly and eloquently set forth. The marvelous worth of the Christian life is celebrated in moving, even rhapsodic, terms, as also in the Epistle to the Hebrews—and with the same purpose: namely, to unite the church in loyalty to Christ at a time when both the unity and the loyalty were being severely tested. This great letter, so thoroughly Pauline although not composed by Paul, was put in first place as a kind of preface. Only in subsequent editions, when this epistle was given another location in the collection and a church name had to be found for it, did it come to be known as "Ephesians." In the beginning it had no title.[3]

This first publication made the letters of Paul so widely and well known that any subsequent large-scale revision of their text in the interest of making them serve still later needs was out of the question. But pseudepigraphy continued to be resorted to. At some time during the first half of the second century an unknown Paulinist composed 1 and 2 Timothy and Titus

---

[3]For evidence here see E. J. Goodspeed, *New Solutions of New Testament Problems* (Chicago: University of Chicago Press, 1927) and *The Meaning of Ephesians* (Chicago: University of Chicago Press, 1933).

in order to refute, in Paul's own name, certain Gnostic views that had gained wide prevalence in the church and were often, even if speciously, defended on the basis of statements of Paul in the older letters. An edition of the collection appeared about 150-75 that incorporated these so-called Pastoral epistles. Another pseudonymous epistle, 3 Corinthians, written with a similar purpose, although not generally accorded canonical status, enjoyed a wide circulation for a while and, in parts of the church at least, the highest esteem.

The examination of such efforts to adjust the Pauline letter collection to uses not dreamed of by Paul himself or even by the first collector makes an interesting study; but since these pseudepigraphs have been thoroughly discredited long ago as sources for the life of Paul, we do not need to consider them further. The post-Pauline character of Ephesians is also very widely recognized. We are thus left with Romans, 1 and 2 Corinthians, Galatians, Philippians, Colossians, 1 and 2 Thessalonians, and Philemon[4] as presumably authentic letters of Paul, coming to us substantially as they left their author's hand. They constitute our only primary sources for the life of Paul. They are manifestly of inestimable value to the student of his ideas and his mind; if they are of less value for the reconstruction of his career, this is only because they happen to say less about the external facts of the apostle's life and work.

III

Pseudepigraphy was not the only method of reinterpreting Paul—of making him relevant to the interests and needs of the church, or of some part of it, a generation or so after his death, and of bringing his authority to bear upon new issues. To be sure, Paul had been a writer of letters; and, especially after a collection of the letters had become widely known, the obvious way to correct or supplement his teaching—or what was being currently represented as his teaching—was to compose additional letters. But Paul had also been a great evangelist and apostle, a founder and leader of churches; a second way of reinterpreting him was the writing of an account of his career. The book of Acts, under one of its aspects, is probably the earliest, and certainly the worthiest, of several of these biographical attempts.

---

[4] Of these, 2 Thessalonians and Colossians are the most questionable.

Note the phrase ''under one of its aspects''; it is important to recognize that Acts is not simply, or even primarily, a life of Paul. This second volume of Luke's work seeks to tell the story of the expansion of Christianity, and Paul is presumably important to the author's purpose only insofar as he has a place in that broader story. Still, there can be no question that Luke has, for whatever reason, a special interest in Paul. Once the Christian movement reaches Gentile soil, it is the line of expansion in which Paul prominently figured that alone engages the writer. Paul's name appears as early as 7:58 and is mentioned again in 8:1. The larger part of chapter 9 is devoted to him. He enters the story again in 11:25-30 and in 12:25. The sixteen chapters that follow 13:1 are concerned entirely with him. It is not too much to say that the latter half of Acts is a narrative of the career of Paul the apostle.

How trustworthy and adequate is that narrative as a source for the life of Paul? We may fairly answer that question by saying that it is, on the whole, no less and no more trustworthy and adequate than the Gospel section of the same author's work as a source for the life of Jesus. To say this, we must recognize, is to make, not a weak and grudging concession, but a strong affirmation of the historical value of Acts. We know that the author of the Gospel of Luke had good sources—two of these, Mark and Q, can be identified, since Matthew also used them.[5] The very fact that two writers, Matthew and Luke, independently of each other, depended chiefly upon these two sources strongly suggests that they were most firmly and widely established in the regard and use of the primitive community and were presumably the two best sources available. Luke also had his own otherwise unknown sources: for example, a document (documents?) rich in parables, now found chiefly in 9:51-18:14, that commends itself as containing not only some of the most significant and beautiful Gospel material but also some of the most reliable and authentic. He must also have had a special source or sources for the first section of his work, which treats of

---

[5]Reflected here is the view of Synoptic Gospel relationships which with variations was current when the former edition of this book appeared in 1950 and which, incidentally, I have not seen sufficient reason to abandon, but which cannot now be said to prevail. In this revised edition I leave the original statement unchanged, for the point I am making here is not involved—namely, that Luke had respectable sources and made responsible use of them, but that he did not hesitate to depart from them on occasion if he saw good reason to do so.

the birth and youth of Jesus. These sources he apparently followed with considerable fidelity, but it can be demonstrated, on the basis of his use of Mark, that he did not hesitate to make changes in the wording to suit his own literary taste; that his selection of material from his sources was affected by his own personal and religious interests (for example, in women and home life, in the poor, in punitive miracles); that he often felt justified in altering details in the stories or sayings he selected for the sake of these same interests; and that he felt no objection to modifying the order of the materials in his sources if his own literary purpose, that is, his own conception of the overall meaning of the materials, suggested another arrangement as more appropriate or effective.

It is fair to assume that the same literary methods were followed in the composition of Acts. There can be no question that the author had some excellent primitive sources—some of them dealing with the early Jerusalem community, others with the church in Antioch, others with the activities of Paul, as, for example, the so-called diary, excerpts from which occasionally appear. It is also indicated that he used these sources carefully and faithfully; but again we may assume that he selected and altered his materials in just the same ways as in the Gospel section. This assumption is confirmed when we note emerging prominently in the Acts narrative the same interests we have previously observed in the Gospel. We must also assume that he arranged his materials in the order that best suited the purpose of his book.

There are at least two respects in which the author may be presumed to have acted with a freer hand in Acts than in the Gospel. One of these is the matter of the *teaching* of the apostle. The Paul of Acts does not write letters—and this omission may have significance[6]—but he does make speeches. Between twenty and twenty-five per cent of the words of Acts 13-28, the section dealing predominantly with Paul, are words put in the mouth of the apostle. Placed end to end, Paul's addresses in Acts would make a document approximately as long as Ephesians. Now these speeches are largely, if not entirely, the composition of the author. He would undoubtedly have shrunk from composing discourses for Jesus (although a later writer was willing to do even this), but he does not hesitate to compose speeches for Paul. Such composition was in line with the current

---

[6]See below, 78; also my book, *Marcion and the New Testament* (Chicago: University of Chicago Press, 1942; rpt. New York: AMS, 1980) 132ff.

practice of historians—such as Thucydides, Livy and Caesar—and involved no infraction of literary ethics. But a recognition of Luke's resort to this practice, however legitimate and well understood by his first readers, will prevent our citing any of Paul's words in Acts as though they were the apostle's own. Both in idea and in literary style the speeches resemble not Paul's work, with which we are fortunately in a position to compare them, but Luke's. This means that for any knowledge we gain of Paul's ideas and the more inward aspects of his personality the letters constitute our only reliable source.

The second respect in which we must suppose the author of Luke-Acts has acted more independently in the Acts section has to do with the *order* of materials. In the Gospel section he incorporated a considerable part of Mark—and, if B. H. Streeter is right, perhaps another complete "gospel." In using such a source as Mark, the author made, as we have seen, a great many characteristic changes, but only occasional, even if quite significant, changes of order. But Mark was already a skillful and well-known *consecutive* account. Now it is generally acknowledged that the original sources did not provide the first Gospel writer with such an account; the arrangement of incidents and teachings in Mark is for the most part his own construction. Jesus' movements back and forth across the Sea of Galilee and around the countryside, with significant words and acts distributed between, represent Mark's—or some Ur-Markus's—way of presenting materials that had come to him piecemeal or in small clusters. Mark had already done this organizing work when Matthew and Luke set their hands to their own tasks, and both show great respect for the way he had done it by following it with great fidelity. But when Luke moved into the field of his second volume, it is likely that no similar work had been done on the traditions of the apostolic age. The writer probably had available only brief accounts of particular episodes; or, perhaps occasionally, of short sequences of episodes, as, for example, of some journey of Paul; or, possibly, longer overlapping accounts written from divergent points of view from which the writer had to make selections. He was thus free to draw more largely upon his own imagination simply because he was forced to do so if he was going to weave all of these scattered materials into a continuous whole. When he wrote Acts, therefore, it is probable that he was more the author and less the compiler than when he wrote Luke; we may confidently believe that he had greater control of the arrangement of his materials and was in large part responsible for it.

As far as Paul's career is concerned, this arrangement was made, inev itably and legitimately, in accordance with Luke's conception of the gen- eral character of that career, its relationships and its consequences. Out of many features of that conception, three are especially important for the student of the life of Paul.

IV

One of these features is a tendency to emphasize the role of Jerusalem in the story of the beginnings of the church. This tendency is by no means limited to Luke-Acts; it appears no less unmistakably in the Fourth Gospel and seems to have been generally characteristic of early Christian apolo- getic as a feature of the effort to commend Christianity to Gentile readers or hearers. The ground for it lay, no doubt, partly in the fact that Jerusalem was the most important Jewish city, the only place in Palestine of which the ordinary person in Asia Minor, Greece or Italy would ever have heard. Thus it seemed the appropriate place for the occurrence of such supremely important events as those that issued in the Christian movement. One could refer to Jerusalem and Judea as the birthplace of Christianity without ex- planation or apology; this was not true of Nazareth, or Capernaum, or even Galilee. But the connection of Christianity with Jerusalem had a more par- ticular value for the writer of Acts. One of his major theses is that Chris- tianity is the continuance of authentic Judaism, that the new covenant validates and fulfills the old. A practical motive for making this point was no doubt to secure for Christianity the protection of the state, which Ju- daism as a *religio licita* enjoyed. Another motive may well have been to refute certain claims concerning Christianity's independence of Judaism to which Marcionites and others later gave wide prevalence—doubtless they were already being made when Acts was composed, whether that was be- tween 90 and 100 or later. "Christianity," Luke is saying in effect, "is not a new religion; it is as old as Moses and the prophets; it is the true Is- rael." But the center of Israel was Jerusalem. It was there that the old Is- rael had decisively rejected its king and its destiny; only there should be born the new Israel, which claimed that king and that destiny. Jerusalem was the symbol of the continuity of Christianity with Judaism, of the ful- fillment of Judaism in the church.

However we understand the reasons for Luke's emphasis upon the role of Jerusalem in the beginnings of the Christian movement, there can be no doubt of the fact of it. We note this already in the Gospel section. That

Jesus' public ministry, except for the last few days of it, took place elsewhere than in Judea was a fact too well established for Luke to doubt or
alter; but he describes the resurrection appearances as occurring in or near
Jerusalem, although both Mark and Matthew clearly place them in Galilee;
and he begins his Gospel, not only in Jerusalem, but even in the temple
there, with an account of the circumstances surrounding the birth of John
the Baptist. Indeed, a large part of the scene of the first two chapters of
Luke is laid in the temple. Jesus is brought to Jerusalem soon after his birth
and is hailed in the temple by Simeon and Anna. Again when he is twelve,
having come to Jerusalem for the Passover, as apparently happened each
year, he remains in the temple for several days after his parents have left,
discussing the meaning of Scripture with the rabbis. There can be no question that one of the primary interests served by the first two chapters of
Luke's Gospel is his interest in emphasizing the connection of Christianity
with Jerusalem, a connection neither Mark nor Q gave him a chance to emphasize within the limits of Jesus' public career.

In Acts this interest in Jerusalem could be more freely expressed, since,
as we have seen, the writer was probably not bound by an earlier consecutive source or by a well-established tradition. As we have already noted,
the resurrection appearances take place in Jeruslaem or its vicinity. The
disciples are warned by the risen Christ "not to depart from Jerusalem,"
but to wait there for the promised Spirit. Jesus' ascension takes place only
a short distance from the city. Indeed, the scene of the first seven chapters
of Acts is laid entirely in or near Jerusalem, often in the temple. Jerusalem
assumes oversight of new communites in Samaria and Syria. The mission
to the Gentiles is authorized there. Paul has his first connection with Christianity in Jerusalem, his missionary career is supported directly by Antioch
but indirectly by Jerusalem, and the whole structure of it is provided by his
periodic journeys to the city. It is there that he is finally arrested and his
active career comes to an end. Not only is Jerusalem the point from which
the worldwide expansion of Christianity takes its start; Jerusalem remains
the center of the whole development, the source of direction and control
in the expanding church.

The second feature of Luke's conception of the beginnings of the church
that is particularly pertinent to the study of the life of Paul has been antic-
ipated in our discussion of the first. It is the view that the Twelve at Jerusalem exercised a careful and authoritative oversight of the entire
Christian church. According to Acts, Paul, as well as other evangelists,

acknowledges the authority of this central council and works under its di
rection. Paul, although perhaps superior in gifts and personal stature, is in
status inferior to the Twelve. They are apostles in virtue of having been
with Christ and being witnesses to the Resurrection. Paul is, so to speak,
ordained to the apostleship by the laying on of hands (13:1-3), and far from
claiming to have seen the Resurrection himself, he appeals to the testimony of the disciples (13:30-31). Paul's vision in chapter 9 takes place after
the Ascension and is of a different order from the resurrection appearances
witnessed by the earlier disciples. These disciples, now established as "the
Twelve," are the real and universally acknowledged authority in the
church. Acts, therefore, leaves the reader with a distinct impression of the
harmony and concord of the primitive community. Problems occasionally
arise, to be sure, especially at first, but they are quickly and effectively
settled by the action of "the apostles and elders." In a word, the catholic
church is, in principle at least, fully in existence, although its seat is still
in Jerusalem.[7] Perhaps a hint of the destined change of locale is intended
in the fact that Paul is finally brought to Rome, and the story of the book
of Acts, having begun in Jerusalem, ends in the Imperial City.

The third feature of the conception of Luke-Acts can be indicated even
more briefly. It is the emphasis the author places upon the politcal innocuousness of the new movement. Paul in the course of his mission is on several occasions haled before Roman officials, but each time the magistrate
finds no fault in him, recognizing that Paul's religion is really Judaism, a
legitimate cult, and that no crime is involved in his practicing and pro-
mulgating it. Paul's enemies are never responsible Gentile officials but are
overzealous and bigoted Jews, false to the true meaning of their own faith
and culture. It is these enemies who attack him in Jerusalem as the end of
his career approaches, and his arrest there by the Roman authorities is really
a protective act. He is heard sympathetically by Felix, Festus and Agrippa,
not to mention Drusilla, the wife of Felix, and Bernice, the sister of
Agrippa. Their final conclusion is that "this man is doing nothing to deserve death or imprisonment," and that if he had not at an earlier stage
appealed to Caesar, he "could have been set free" (26:31-32). There can
be little question that Luke's silence as to the fate of this appeal is a con-

---

[7]For a much fuller and very discerning summary of this aspect of the "theory"
of the writer of Acts see B. S. Easton, *The Purpose of Acts* (London: S.P.C.K.,
1926) esp. 9-22.

sequence of his unwillingness to conclude his book with the story of its failure. The book ends with Paul still awaiting his trial before the emperor.

That all of these features of the Acts account of the primitive church represent in some measure the *theory* of the writer rather than the character of the original facts is generally acknowledged. The only question is: In what measure? To what extent must the student of the life of Paul make allowances for these theoretical presuppositions of the author of Luke-Acts? That question can be answered only on the basis of a careful comparison of his account with Paul's letters.

Chapter II

The Use of Our Sources

We have seen that both of our sources for the life of Paul—a collection of his letters and the book of Acts—come to us in forms dating from not earlier than the last decade of the first century, or a generation after Paul's death, and that some allowance must be made for the effects of the interests, needs and beliefs of that generation upon the work both of the collector and editor of the letters and of the author of Acts. Both had in hand important primitive materials—the collector, some genuine letters of the apostle; the author, some early traditions about him—but both were interested in making these materials serve a later purpose. We have also seen, however, that while the contribution of the collector (if we leave out of account the writing of the general epistle known later as Ephesians) can be limited to the selecting and arranging of the letters, to the combining of some letters or fragments, and to the kind of occasional rewriting, interpolation, and omission that all editors practice, the author of Acts was in position to deal with his Pauline materials with a freer hand. This does not mean that he dealt with them less honestly and conscientiously; it means only that they were probably of such kind—fragmentary accounts of Paul—that to make something unified and coherent out of them required the use of a good deal of imagination. Such imaginative reconstruction is of course involved in any historical writing, but it is always subject to testing and retesting and becomes indubitably true only when the relevant facts are all known, and when they all firmly support the proposed reconstruction and no other. Till then its hypothetical character must be clearly and constantly borne in mind. Such is the position in which the Acts story of the career of Paul has always stood, and stands now. Thus, of our two sources, the letters of Paul are obviously and incomparably the more trustworthy.

The truth in principle of this last statement no serious student of Paul's life is likely to deny, but its meaning in practice is not so widely or so clearly seen. With that ''meaning in practice''—that is, with the way our sources should be actually used—we are now concerned.

I

We may begin by distinguishing again between the thought, the personal character and the religious experience of the apostle on the one hand, and ordinary biographical data on the other—what might be called the ''internal'' and the ''external'' spheres of Paul's life. This distinction is convenient because it enables us to dispose quickly of the question of methodology as regards the recovery of the internal facts. Paul's own letters, besides being his own, are so rich in indications of what kind of man he was and of what was going on in his mind and heart that no one would seriously argue that Acts is in the same class with them as a source for the internal facts. One may go further than this and say that even the naive reader of the New Testament, who would not hesitate to quote from the Acts account of Paul's speech before Agrippa in the same breath with something from the letter to the Romans, will really have derived his or her picture of the personality of the apostle and a conception of the apostle's message from the letters, even though the reader may not recognize that this is true. The impression of these inner facts, which the letters of Paul make on any faithful reader, is so vivid and strong that even a naive trust in the adequacy and accuracy of Acts is not enough to make it a real competitor in that sphere. Actually the Paul of Acts is in important respects a quite different kind of man and has quite different ideas from the Paul of the letters. The informed and disinterested student sees this and simply disregards Acts as a source for the inner life of Paul; others, either consciously or unconsciously, try to harmonize Acts with the letters. But even for these students, the real source for Paul, that is, for Paul's personality and thought, is *Paul;* and if pressed, they would probably acknowledge that this is true.

A problem arises only when we move from Paul's character and ideas to his life in the more external sense, for in this sphere the letters do not provide us with any coherent picture of the facts. To be sure, there are a few clear autobiographical statements—and, as we shall see, more can be inferred from them than is usually recognized—but we could not write anything like a circumstantial "life" of Paul from the data his own quite incidental statements provide. Acts, on the other hand, does give us a somewhat circumstantial, even if summary, biographical sketch. The impression made by the *life* of Paul in Acts is quite as vivid and strong in comparison with the letters as is the impression of his *personality* and *thought* made by the letters in comparison with Acts. The consequence is that while we tend to harmonize Acts with the letters as regards the inner facts of Paul's life, we tend to harmonize the letters with Acts as regards the outer. Neither instance of harmonization, of course, can be justified; but whereas the first is relatively innocuous, since the letters are given their true importance in the process, the second is seriously distorting. After all, the reason we are justified in giving primacy to the letters as regards Paul's inner life is not that the letters give a more forceful and vivid impression of that life than does Acts, but rather that the letters represent a firsthand, and Acts a secondhand, source. But the letters remain our only firsthand source for the outer facts, too, even though they happen not to say as much about them as Acts does. The distinction between primary and secondary sources in this case is of such importance that we can justly say that a fact only suggested in the letters has a status which even the most unequivocal statement of Acts, if not otherwise supported, cannot confer. We may, with proper caution, use Acts to supplement the autobiographical data of the letters, but never to correct them. Let us see how the application of this principle works out.

II

It is likely to come as something of a surprise to any of us to realize the extent to which the conventional picture of the life of Paul is dependent upon Acts alone. The preceding chapter indicated the major features of that familiar picture in these terms: A Jew with the Jewish name of Saul, born in Tarsus of Cilicia, educated in Jerusalem at the feet of Gamaliel, a persecutor of the church in Judea, converted to Christianity "on the road to Damascus," making three great missionary journeys which took him from Antioch in Syria to regions as far west as Macedonia and Greece, finally arrested on the last of a number to visits of Jerusalem, as a Roman citizen appealing to Caesar after several hearings before local magistrates, arriving finally in Rome for his trial and presumably his martyrdom. Now it is interesting to observe that not one of these statements could be made on the basis of the letters, although several of them secure real support there. As they stand, however, they rest only upon the testimony of Acts. It may be useful to consider them briefly, one by one, applying the principle of criticism just stated.

First, then, the statement that Paul was a Jew named Saul. Here we need only observe that, while we cannot be as certain of Paul's Jewish name as of his Jewishness, we can be virtually sure of both. Our knowledge of Paul's being a Jew rests not only upon the general character of the letters as indicating a Jewish author but also upon a number of explicit assertions in the letters (for example, Rom. 11:1; Phil. 3:5; 2 Cor. 11:22). That Paul was a Jew admits of no doubt whatever. We cannot feel the same assurance about his having been named Saul, since for this datum we must depend solely upon Acts. Still, we are justified in feeling great confidence in its truth. We know that Paul as a Jew would be all but certain to have a Jewish name as well as his Roman name. Since his family regarded itself as being of the tribe of Benjamin (Phil. 3:5; Rom. 11:1), "Saul" would be a likely choice. There is no competing name anywhere in the tradition, and the invention of such a name would have served no discernible interest of the author of Luke-Acts. Likewise, since we cannot point to any occasion in Paul's correspondence where a reference to his Jewish name seems called for, the silence of the letters on this point has no apparent significance. For all these reasons—so obvious that they have been stated only for the sake of illustrating a method—we are justified in accepting this item from Acts as supplementing the Pauline letter data.

The same thing can be said about the second item—Paul's birth in Tarsus. This, too, rests only upon the testimony of Acts (22:3). But again there is no obvious reason why Paul should have mentioned it and no plausible reason why Luke should have invented it (as a matter of fact, he would probably have preferred that Paul come from Jerusalem), and there is no competing suggestion.[1] That Paul was born in Tarsus is in line with the general impression the letters give that their author was an extra-Palestinian Jew, as well as with his apparent indication in Gal. 1:21 that Cilicia was one of the early fields of his evangelistic work. Although, then, we can be fully sure only that Paul was a Hellenistic Jew, for this is all the

---

[1]One may disregard as too late the statement in Jerome that Paul came from Gischala in Galilee to Tarsus (*On Philemon* 23; *De Viris Illustribus* V).

letters tell us, we can be reasonably certain also that he was Saul of Tarsus in Cilicia.

When we come to the next item, however—his education in Jerusalem at the feet of Gamaliel—the reliability of Acts is by no means so clear. Two important differences between the status of this and the status of the foregoing items must be observed. The first is that Paul's complete silence about this connection with the noted Jewish teacher must be interpreted in light of the fact that on several occasions in his letters we would expect him to mention it. As we have already noted, Paul more than once boasts of the authenticity and orthodoxy of his Judaism and of his zeal for the religion of his fathers (see Gal. 1:14, in addition to the passages already cited in this chapter). Why does he say nothing of his education in Jerusalem at the feet of this distinguished rabbi? The second reason for doubt about this statement of Luke-Acts is that it *does* answer to, and serve, one of the important interests of the author: the interest in Christianity as the continuation and fulfullment of authentic Judaism and in the city of Jerusalem as the place where the transition took place. If Paul were in fact a pupil of Gamaliel, that fact wonderfully suited the purposes of Luke. Such an observation is, of course, not a decisive argument against the alleged fact but, especially when taken in connection with Paul's silence, does serve to cast some doubt upon it. That Paul knew something—perhaps a great deal—about rabbinical theology and exegesis is clear from the letters, but such knowledge could be acquired wherever there was a well-established Jewish community. The acknowledgment of it does not require either Jerusalem or Gamaliel. This is one of a class of items that we are not justified in denying, but of which we must be gravely doubtful.[2]

The reasons for this doubt about his education in Jerusalem appear even stronger when we consider it in connection with the next two items, which almost have to be examined together—a persecutor of the church in Judea, who was converted to Christianity on the road to Damascus. Here we are forced to recognize a real conflict between the Acts story and the clear meaning of Paul's own words, and therefore must reject the Acts story out of hand. Not that there is any question about Paul's having persecuted the church; a number of references in the letters place that beyond doubt (see, for example, 1 Cor. 15:9; Gal. 1:13). But Acts makes much of the fact that

---

[2]For other comments on this issue see 54, 118.

the scene of this persecuting activity was Jerusalem and Judea. Paul does not tell us, in so many words, the *place* of this activity, but he does make clear that this place was *not* Jerusalem or Judea. How else can we interpret his words in Gal. 1:22-23, written concerning a time three or more years after his conversion: "I was still not known by sight to the churches of Christ in Judea; they only heard it said, 'He who once persecuted us is now preaching the faith he once tried to destroy' "?

Indeed, the whole passage (Gal. 1:11-24) not only suggests but demands the view that Paul was living, not in Jerusalem, but elsewhere—probably at Damascus—immediately before, at the time of, and for at least three years after, his conversion. Paul says, "I returned to Damacus" (vs. 17) as one might say, "I returned home." Then he continues, "After three years I went up to Jerusalem to visit Cephas, and remained with him fifteen days" (vs. 18)—a statement hardly applicable to the city where he lived. This and the reference in 2:1 to journeys to Jerusalem clearly indicate *visits,* and indeed such is the term ordinarily used when this passage in Galatians is discussed. But in Acts, Paul does not "visit" Jerusalem three years after his conversion; he *returns* there quite soon afterward, as one would expect him to do. After telling of Paul's forced departure from Damascus, Luke says without any previous explanation: "When he had come to Jerusalem" (Acts 9:26; cf. 22:17). Of course that is where he would go! Did he not live there? Had he not left there only a short time before on this errand to Damacus? Luke says,

> When he had come to Jerusalem he attempted to join the disciples; and they were all afraid of him, for they did not believe that he was a disciple. But Barnabas took him, and brought him to the apostles, and declared to them how on the road he had seen the Lord, who spoke to him, and how at Damascus he had preached boldly in the name of Jesus. So he went in and out among them at Jerusalem, preaching boldly in the name of the Lord. (9:26-29a)

The Acts story hangs together, but it simply does not hang together with Paul's own statement, and no amount of ingenuity can remove the egregious contradictions. Paul says that after his conversion, he "did not confer with flesh and blood"; Acts tells of his conferences with Ananias and others at Damascus. Paul says, "I did not . . . go up to Jerusalem to those who were apostles before me"; Acts says that he did precisely that. Two utterly different and quite irreconcilable conceptions of what happened lie under the Acts account just quoted and the following words of Paul:

Then after three years I went up to Jerusalem to visit Cephas, and remained with him fifteen days. But I saw none of the other apostles except James the Lord's brother. (In what I am writing to you, before God, I do not lie!) Then I went into the regions of Syria and Cilicia. And I was still not known by sight to the churches of Christ in Judea. (Gal. 1:18-22)

Sometimes the scholars argue as to why Paul felt constrained to take a solemn oath to the truth of his statement here. I am tempted to suggest that he did so because he had some premonition that most of the books to be written about him in the centuries afterward were going to say to him in effect, "You are wrong about this, Paul. Of course you are not deliberately lying, but quite obviously you are mistaken. For the Acts of the Apostles gives a quite different story. It was written, we have good reason to believe, by Luke, who was a traveling companion of yours and therefore, you will agree, could hardly have been mistaken on a point like this." As if to forestall such an answer, Paul took a solemn oath, but certainly to little avail; nine out of ten of the "lives of Paul" have preferred Luke's version.

The detail on which the two accounts of his conversion agree is that it occurred in or near Damascus. Paul's statement implies this clearly: "I returned to Damascus." We may be sure that this same fact was indicated by Luke's sources. It did not occur to him to doubt it, but since it did not suit his conception of where Paul resided, he must account for it. How did it happen that Paul, who for years had been living in Jerusalem as a pupil of Gamaliel and had been currently engaged in harassing the Christians there, was in Damascus at the time of his conversion? It is likely that the story of Paul's going to Damascus with letters from the high priest to bring believers back to Jerusalem for trial or punishment represents the author's ingenious surmise in answer to that question. Given as facts that Paul at the time of his conversion was engaged in a most violent effort to destroy the church at *Jerusalem,* but that his conversion itself, as well as the persecuting activity that immediately preceded it, took place at *Damascus,* Luke's explanation is probably the best possible. The author's problem here was quite similar to the problem he faced at the beginning of his Gospel as regards the place of Jesus' birth.[3] There he had to account for the fact that

---

[3]This similarity has been frequently noticed. See Alfred Loisy, *Les Actes des Apotres* (Paris: Nourry, 1920) 390; M. S. Enslin, "Paul and Gamaliel," *Journal of Religion* 7 (1927): 360-75.

Jesus, who he knew must have been born in Bethlehem of Judea, was represented by his sources, or at least by some of the best of them, as being from Nazareth. Here he must explain why Paul, who he knew must have had his residence and headquarters in Jerusalem, was known by his sources to have begun his Christian career in Damascus. In each case an element in his *conception* is in apparent contradiction with a fact in the tradition. In each case he makes what seems to him to be a reasonable surmise—a census in Luke and letters of extradition in Acts. Although these letters are much more credible than the census "of the whole world," the Acts story has its difficulties. Why should Damascene Christians be brought back to Jerusalem? Is it likely that the political authorities in Damascus would have gone as far in their cooperation with the religious authority in Jerusalem as the Acts story envisages? It is usually answered that Paul was seeking *Jerusalem* believers who had fled to Damascus and were therefore subject to extradition as escaped criminals.[4] But the Acts statement simply does not lend itself to that interpretation: "Saul . . . went to the high priest and asked him for letters to the synagogues at Damascus, so that if he found any belonging to the Way, men or women, he might bring them bound to Jerusalem." Clearly he does not know of particular Jerusalemite believers who have fled to Damascus; he does not even know, apparently, that there are Christians there at all. And even if he found persons subject to extradition, would letters, "to the synagogues at Damascus" be enough to enable Paul to apprehend them and to bring them back to Jerusalem? Besides these questions, we may ask whether it is not more likely that if the Sanhedrin in Jerusalem was concerned about the spread of Christianity to foreign cities, it would have warned the Jewish communities in those cities of the peril and urged them to take strong action. We conclude, then, that the Acts story in 9:1-2, while not incredible, is improbable. It has every mark of being a skillful way of accounting for a strange fact—the conversion of a Jerusalemite Jew in Damasus. The author ventures to take some liberty even with the datum of his sources about Damascus itself: Paul's conversion takes place as he "approached Damascus."

But if Luke's conception of Paul's life as centered in Jerusalem has had the effect of distorting what his sources probably gave him as to the locale of Paul's conversion and of his attacks upon the church immediately be-

---

[4]Cf. 1 Maccabees 15:21; Josephus *Antiquities* XIV. 10.1.

fore, we are bound to allow even more definitely for the possibility that
the story of Paul's education in Jerusalem is also the creation of that same
conception. That story may represent Luke's way of explaining how it
happened that one who was born in Tarsus in Cilicia was later a resident
of Jerusalem.

III

No feature of Paul's career is more familiar than the three great missionary journeys in which the active years of the apostle's life were spent,
each journey beginning from Antioch or Jerusalem and ending there. We
are likely to speak of the missionary journeys as we do of the crucifixion
of Jesus—facts both undoubted and indubitable. Maps designed to represent the scene of Paul's activities are regularly marked by long lines of dots,
dashes and asterisks that indicate his routes on the three missionary journeys. The final journey to Rome, which also starts from Palestine, is similarly marked.

But this way of visualizing and representing the career of Paul is based
entirely upon Acts, with no support from the letters whatsoever. Not that
the conception of Paul as a traveler is absent from the letters: Paul is constantly speaking of trips, remembered or contemplated, and the very word
apostle suggests, among other things, the traveler. But the pattern of the
three great journeys does not emerge in Paul's letters. The recognition that
this pattern can be derived only from Acts does not, as we have seen, mean
that it needs to be rejected (*Tarsus* and *Saul* are also found only in Acts).
That recognition, however, does require that we scrutinize the pattern
carefully in the light of what the letters do say and of what we know of the
interests and character of Luke-Acts.

We may begin by reminding ourselves again that the letters of Paul reveal not the slightest awareness on his part that he is engaged in great journeys. To be sure, he knows that his work began in Syria and Cilicia and
has moved westward (cf. Rom. 15:19); it is true also that he regards the
founding of churches in new places and the visiting and revisiting of
churches he has founded as being of the very essence of his work. But there
is no sign that he regards these small journeys as being parts of a series of
big journeys, each of which had its beginning and its end in Antioch or
Jerusalem.

This is not a mere argument from silence, for Paul refers to visits to
Jerusalem, if not also to Antioch. But these are *visits;* they are not *returns*.

He never "goes back" to Jerusalem; normally he "goes up." He goes each time because he has some reason to go, not, as when one returns home, because he has no reason longer to stay away. In Acts we get the impression of Paul as based in Antioch and Jerusalem, visiting the field of his work; in the letters we find him based in his field and visiting Antioch and Jerusalem. When Paul in Rom. 15:19-29 tells of his contemplated trip to Rome, he does so in a manner that plainly indicates his own complete autonomy. He is going to Rome and then to Spain, "by God's will" as he has been given directly to know it, and not because he has in any sense been sent or directed there by Antioch or Jerusalem. To be sure, he must first go up to Jerusalem—but not to complete the "third missionary journey"! He must go to take some money his churches have raised for the more needy Christians in that city. The trip represents for him, not the natural and necessary conclusion of a prearranged itinerary, but a regrettable interruption in the working out of his plans.

This matter of the relation of Paul's work to Jerusalem as it is represented in the letters and in Acts calls for several chapters of its own. We can at least note here that the missionary journey scheme suits perfectly the conception of the author of Acts that Paul throughout his career worked closely with the older communities of Syria and Palestine and more or less under the authority of the Twelve. It seems certain that the visualization of Paul's life as an apostle in terms of three great missionary tours represents a later way of seeing and interpreting a career that originally did not appear so at all. If you had stopped Paul on the streets of Ephesus and said to him, "Paul, which of your missionary journeys are you on now?" he would have looked at you blankly without the remotest idea of what was in your mind. No one should understand this to mean that Paul thought of himself as a settled minister or teacher anywhere; he was always expecting to move into a new field when his work in the old one was done. But that he saw his career as characterized by a series of movements from Jerusalem and back again is surely very unlikely.

IV

We may deal briefly with the final items in our sketch: Paul's arrest in Jerusalem, his trials in Caesarea and his voyage to Rome. All of these items are derived only from Acts; but Paul's silence with respect to them has no significance, if for no other reason, because it is possible that every one of his surviving letters had been written before the final events, whatever they were, occurred. His letter to the Romans, however, prepares us not only to expect this last visit to Jerusalem but also for the difficulties he encountered there (15:25-32). He wrote that letter when he was on the point of embarking for Jerusalem, and he clearly indicates his awareness of the dangers he will incur "from the unbelievers in Judea." Thus the letters to some extent support the Acts story of what happened in Jerusalem.

The letter to the Romans also informs us of Paul's desire to go to Rome. A strong and fairly early tradition confirms the Acts story that he did in fact finally reach that city, adding that he suffered martyrdom there. We must be somewhat less sure that he reached Rome as a consequence of an appeal to the emperor, although there is no reason to distrust this detail. His Roman citizenship, which provided the basis for the appeal, is not mentioned by Paul himself, and it does fit nicely with Luke's conception of the political innocuousness of Christianity and the cosmopolitan character and interests of Paul. The only positive argument against it is Paul's reference (2 Cor. 11:25) to having been "three times . . . beaten with rods," an official Roman punishment. However, this is far from conclusive (the magistrates may not have known about Paul's Roman citizenship or believed his claims).[5] We are likely to feel a little more doubt about the formal hearings before the Sanhedrin, Felix, Festus and Agrippa. Since Paul's speeches are clearly the composition of the author of Acts, the occasions of one or more of them may be his creation too. We cannot forget in that connection the fact that Luke alone among the Gospels tells of trials of Jesus before Herod—who, like Agrippa later, happened to be near—as well as before Pilate. In a word, although there is every reason for trusting the essential historicity of the final chapters of Acts, there is ample reason for being doubtful about the details.

The purpose of this chapter has been, not to give a complete sketch of Paul's life, but to illustrate a principle of criticism by applying it at various points to our sources. In this process, however, a very rough account of his life has emerged: Paul, whose Jewish name was Saul, was a Hellenistic Jew, probably born in Tarsus, but later residing in Damascus. There he

---

[5]Lake and Cadbury suggest that although Roman citizens were probably not scourged in the course of trial or examination, it is possible that scourging was allowed as a punishment after condemnation. See F. J. Foakes-Jackson and Kirsopp Lake, *The Beginnings of Christianity*, pt. 1 (London: Macmillan & Co., 1933) 4:283.

participated actively in the persecution of the Christian movement until he himself became an adherent of it. He became a vigorous evangelist of the new faith, first in Syria, later in Cilicia, Galatia, Asia, Macedonia and Greece. We lose sight of him, so far as our primary sources go, as he is leaving Corinth on a trip to Jerusalem, but it is not improbable that he was arrested there and that, having appealed to Caesar and having been sent to Rome for a final hearing of his case, he ended his life as a martyr to his faith.

Let us now turn to a more detailed discussion of that part of his career that lies between his conversion and his departure for Jerusalem on his last visit—a visit that, as things worked out, marked the end of his active life as an apostle.

Part 2

The Career of the Apostle

Chapter III

The Story in the Letters

We have noted more than once the fact that Paul's letters, although they tell us much about himself and his thought, provide us with very little information about the external facts of his career. It is this omission, altogether natural in letters and to be expected, that accounts for our tendency to rely upon Acts except at the points where one of Paul's occasional remarks absolutely requires that we recognize an error. Many writers seem to proceed on the assumption that for some reason Luke was more accurately informed on matters concerning which Paul happens to be silent than on matters concerning which Paul happens to have spoken. One of them once said to me, "But if we cannot rely confidently upon Acts, what is left us? We would not be able to write a life of Paul at all"—as though such a consideration had anything to do with the question of the reliability of Acts! Suppose we are not in position to write a life of Paul in the sense of a dependable, consecutive and somewhat circumstantial account of his career; are we not in precisely that position with respect to the life of Jesus? As I noted in the first chapter, we are in danger of allowing the accidental fact that only Luke wrote about Paul, whereas he and several others wrote about Jesus, to blind us to the possibility that the practical and literary purposes of the author of Acts or his predecessors have had effects upon the traditions they received not less considerable than the effects which similar purposes are generally acknowledged to have had upon the earliest traditions of Jesus' life. In other words, we lack the controls for the life of Paul that the several Gospels provide for the life of Jesus.

It would be a mistake, however, to suppose that we are altogether deficient in this respect. The letters of Paul give us more information than is commonly recognized and provide us at certain important points with an effective check on the Lukan account.

I

Let us imagine for a moment that only Paul's letters had come down to us, that the book of Acts had either never been written or had perished without leaving a trace—in that case, what could we know about Paul? It is clear that we could know as much about the personality and thought of Paul as we can know now; but what about his life in the external sense? We have already noted what his letters reveal as to his life before he became a Christian, as well as their silence after he leaves for Jerusalem on what was almost certainly his final visit. What do the letters tell us of his life between these limits? What can we gather from his letters as to the length, locale and movement of his career as an apostle?

As to its length, it is important to recognize that the letters provide us with our most important information, even if the testimony of Acts is accepted without reservation, since Acts is exceedingly vague about *intervals*. Luke tells us that Paul once lived a year and a half at Corinth and that he once made a two-year stay at Ephesus (Acts 19:10; but cf. 20:31), and intervals of three months are mentioned a time or two. Because his narrative is liberally interspersed with such phrases as "after many days" or "after some days," these occasional more definite statements are robbed of value as far as the chronological reconstruction of Paul's career is concerned. The conventional chronology of Paul's life is arrived at by harmonizing *Paul's* intervals with Luke's *incidents*. But we are now supposing for a moment that we do not have Luke's incidents; could anything like a chronological pattern be derived from the letters alone?

The most important relevant autobiographical material in the letters is brief enough to be presented in full.

> You have heard of my former life in Judaism, how I persecuted the church of God violently and tried to destroy it; and I advanced in Judaism beyond many of my own age among my people, so extremely zealous was I for the traditions of my fathers. But when he who had set me apart before I was born, and had called me through his grace, was pleased to reveal his Son to me, in order that I might preach him among the Gentiles, I did not confer with flesh and blood, nor did I go up to Jerusalem to those who were apostles before me, but I went away into Arabia; and again I returned to Damascus.

Then after three years I went up to Jerusalem to visit Cephas, and remained with him fifteen days. But I saw none of the other apostles except James the Lord's brother. (In what I am writing to you, before God, I do not lie!) Then I went into the regions of Syria and Cilicia. And I was still not known by sight to the churches of Christ in Judea; they only heard it said, "He who once persecuted us is now preaching the faith he once tried to destroy." And they glorified God because of me.

Then after fourteen years I went up again to Jerusalem with Barnabas, taking Titus along with me. I went up by revelation; and I laid before them (but privately before those who were of repute) the gospel which I preach among the Gentiles, lest somehow I should be running or had run in vain. But even Titus, who was with me, was not compelled to be circumcised, though he was a Greek. But because of false brethren secretly brought in, who slipped in to spy out our freedom which we have in Christ Jesus, that they might bring us into bondage—to them we did not yield submission even for a moment, that the truth of the gospel might be preserved for you. And from those who were reputed to be something (what they were makes no difference to me; God shows no partiality)—those, I say, who were of repute added nothing to me; but on the contrary, when they saw that I had been entrusted with the gospel to the uncircumcised, just as Peter had been entrusted with the gospel to the circumcised (for he who worked through Peter for the mission to the circumcised worked through me also for the Gentiles), and when they perceived the grace that was given to me, James and Cephas and John, who were reputed to be pillars, gave to me and Barnabas the right hand of fellowship, that we should go to the Gentiles and they to the circumcised; only they would have us remember the poor, which very thing I was eager to do. (Gal. 1:13-2:10)

Now concerning the contribution for the saints: as I directed the churches of Galatia, so you also are to do. On the first day of every week, each of you is to put something aside and save, as he may prosper, so that contributions need not be made when I come. And when I arrive, I will send those whom you accredit by letter to carry your gift to Jerusalem. If it seems advisable that I should go also, they will accompany me. (1 Cor. 16:1-4)

Now, since I no longer have any room for work in these regions, and since I have longed for many years to come to you, I hope to see you in passing as I go to Spain, and to be sped on my journey there by you, once I have enjoyed your company for a little. At present, however, I am going to Jerusalem with aid for the saints. For Macedonia and Achaia have been pleased to make some contribution for the poor among the saints at Jerusalem; they were pleased to do it, and indeed they are in debt to them, for if the Gentiles have come to share in their spiritual blessings, they ought also to be of service to them in material blessing. When therefore I have completed this, and have delivered to them what has been raised, I shall go on by way of you to Spain; and I know that when I come to you I shall come in the fullness of the blessing of Christ.

I appeal to you, brethren, by our Lord Jesus Christ and by the love of the Spirit, to strive together with me in your prayers to God on my behalf, that I may be delivered from the unbelievers in Judea, and that my service for Jerusalem may be acceptable to the saints, so that by God's will I may come to you with joy and be refreshed in your company. (Rom. 15:23-32)

Reducing this to outline form, we have something like the following:

I. Conversion in Damacus—Gal. 1:15-17
II. Three years or more, spent largely or entirely in Syria and Arabia—Gal. 1:17-18
III. First visit to Jerusalem after the conversion (''acquaintance'') and departure for Syria and Cilicia—Gal. 1:18-21
IV. Fourteen years, presumably passed in activity as an apostle—Gal. 2:1[1]
V. Second visit to Jerusalem (''conference'')—Gal. 2:1-10
VI. Activity in churches of Galatia, Asia, Macedonia and Greece, especially in connection with raising the offering for the poor at Jerusalem—Gal. 1:10; 1 Cor. 16:1-4 (also 2 Cor. 8-9); Rom. 15:25-32
VII. Final visit to Jerusalem (''offering'') (1 Cor. 16:4; Rom. 15:25-32)

---

[1]A generation ago many students of the Pauline chronology (including myself for a time) would have affirmed at this point an eleven-year interval rather than one of fourteen years. They argued that the ἔπειτα in this verse looked back to the conversion rather than to the ''acquaintance'' visit. But this is certainly not the most natural way to read the text, and that view, so far as I know, has been generally abandoned. I had become very doubtful of it when the first edition of this book appeared, and since then I have rejected it as extremely unlikely.

In the two articles mentioned in the preface, where I defended the now rejected view, I proposed that the revelation Paul speaks of in 2 Cor. 12:1-4 as occurring fourteen years before he was then writing was identical to the revelation referred to in Gal. 1:15f. But considerations brought forth by many critics and my own further reflection soon led me to see the extreme unlikelihood, if not the impossibility, of this identification, and before the first edition of this book appeared, I had abandoned it. If the Corinthians passage could be taken as an allusion

Before examining the significance of these items, let us note briefly a rather curious fact to which this outline as a whole calls attention. This is the fact that whether we consult Paul's letters or Acts with a view to reconstructing Paul's career as a apostle, the materials furnished us require that we organize it with reference to visits to Jerusalem. We have seen that Luke, as Burton Scott Easton puts it, "gives a Jerusalem frame to all of Paul's ministry, from his departure from Damascus to his final arrest."[2] We have accounted for this frame, as Easton does also, by certain elements in the "theory" of Luke-Acts. But now we note that most of Paul's own references to events in his career as an apostle emphasize his relations with that same city. There are differences, however: Paul mentions three visits and Luke five; but, much more important, Paul is concerned for the most part with showing his independence of Jerusalem and mentions his visits, at least those noted in Galatians, to demonstrate their limited number, meaning and effect, whereas Luke represents Paul as being gladly subordinate to Jerusalem. The fact that Paul mentions these visits, however, reminds us that this matter of Paul's relations with Jerusalem was a matter of controversy, not only in the period of the Marcionite controversy and, earlier, in the period of Luke-Acts, but also within Paul's lifetime. Paul's own attitude toward the apostles in Jerusalem was almost certainly somewhat ambiguous, a mixture of loyalty and respect on the one hand and, on the other, of resistance to any assumption on their part of superior status or authority. Marcion and his predecessors emphasized exclusively one element in this compound and Luke the other, but the issue of the number and nature of Paul's contacts with Jerusalem was important from first to last. Paul says there were only three visits and that they had the purposes indicated in our outline by the terms "acquaintance," "conference" and "offering."

Now this last statement is bound to draw the objection that it goes beyond the evidence: Paul, to be sure, *mentions* only three visits, but he says nothing, one may argue, to indicate that there were not others. The point is crucial. The whole answer to the question whether an inclusive and coherent, even if quite summary, pattern of the length and course of Paul's career as an apostle can be gathered from the letters alone depends upon whether this objection is sound. I believe it is *not* sound. Paul's language

---

to the conversion experience, it would obviously give absolutely decisive support to the chronology I am now defending, but that chronology has never depended upon the interpretation of the passage.

[2]B. S. Easton, *The Purpose of Acts* (London: S. P. C. K., 1926) 19.

in the passages quoted can reasonably be taken to mean not simply three visits but three visits only.

II

We may hope for general agreement that when Paul "went up again to Jerusalem" after "fourteen years" (Gal. 2:1), he was making only his second visit. His whole purpose in this passage in Galatians requires that he be accurate on this point. That he is being careful in his statement appears not only in its definiteness but also in the oath he takes to its truth (1:20). Occasionally it is suggested that he may have been mistaken; perhaps he was forgetting a trip or two. But this suggestion is rarely made, and never with much conviction. Paul would hardly have made an error so egregious or one that would have laid him so open to opponents who apparently were representing his relations with Jerusalem in somewhat the same way as Luke-Acts later represents them. No, it can be known, as surely as such facts can ever be known, that when he went up to Jerusalem "fourteen years later" (V in the outline), he had been up only once before since his conversion.

But on what grounds can we assume that there were no visits to Jerusalem between this second visit and the final one referred to, in anticipation, in 1 Cor. 16:4 and Rom. 15:25-32? The answer here involves our considering the meaning and purpose of the offering that provided the urgent occasion of this final visit.[3]

It is clear that when Paul wrote the fifteenth chapter of Romans, he wished he could at once take a ship for Rome. He tells his readers that he has "for many years" longed to see them, and we have no difficulty in sensing the relief and pleasure with which he now recognizes that his work in Macedonia, Greece, Asia, and elsewhere to the east is in a condition that permits his fulfilling this longtime desire. He cannot go immediately, however; he must deliver in Jerusalem the money that for some time—perhaps as long as three or four years—he has been engaged in raising among his Gentile churches for the poor of the Jerusalem church. 1 Cor. 16:3-4 lets us see that Paul has hoped to avoid this journey and the consequent postponement of his voyage to Rome; he speaks there of his *sending* "those

---

[3]See also Paul S. Minear, "The Jerusalem Fund and the Pauline Chronology," *Anglican Theological Review* 25 (1943): 389 ff. The importance of the offering in this connection is noted in the two articles mentioned in the preface, but it deserves more emphasis than it receives there.

whom you accredit by letter to carry your gift to Jerusalem." Even then, however, he recognizes that he may have to go with them: "If it seems advisable that I go also, they will accompany me." Rom. 15:31-32 tells us that Paul's reluctance to go to Jerusalem is caused not only by his dislike of postponing by many months his visit to Rome but also by his awareness that this trip to Jerusalem involves real danger; he asks that his readers "strive together with me in your prayers to God on my behalf, that I may be delivered from the unbelievers in Judea." (We have already noted that the Acts story of what happened in Jerusalem is fully in line with these forebodings.) But in spite of all this, Paul decides that he cannot avoid this trip. He must go.

Why did Paul feel this great obligation? Why did he feel that he had to go to Jerusalem in spite of the possible loss of his liberty or his life and the certain delay in carrying out a cherished purpose? There can be but one answer to that question—the great symbolic significance of the offering he has just raised. This significance is at least hinted in Rom. 15:31b, where Paul asks the Roman church to pray that the "service for Jerusalem may be acceptable to the saints." He can hardly feel such great anxiety that the offering be simply accepted; what he wants is that it be accepted with full and cordial recognition of its significance. That significance is clear: he hopes that this offering will have the effect of bringing peace to the church, of healing the terrible schism between Jerusalem and the Gentile churches (at least *his* churches) which has distressed him and has embarrassed and impeded his work for a long time.

Now the only other place (that is, besides 1 and 2 Corinthians and Romans) in Paul's letters where a collection for Jerusalem is mentioned is Gal. 2:1-10. There Paul is describing his conference with the leaders of the Jerusalem church over this same issue and how it might be settled. He tells us that this conference ended with James, Cephas and John acknowledging his apostleship and his authority among the Gentile churches and stipulating only that Paul and his churches should "remember the poor" (obviously the poor of the Jerusalem church); "which very thing," Paul adds, "I was eager to do."

There are three, and only three, ways in which this stipulation can be understood. (a) The first is as a reference to a regular, more or less constant, effort on Paul's part to raise and send money to Jerusalem, which he is now asked to continue and which he expresses himself as eager to do. (b) The second is as a reference to some special collection for Jerusalem that antedates the offering being raised in the period of the Corinthian letters. (c) The third is as a reference to this offering. There are no other alternatives.

The first of them is usually chosen: the passage is taken to refer to a common practice of the apostle and the Gentile churches. But there is absolutely no evidence of the existence of such a practice in the letters or, for that matter, in Acts. The only mention of a collection in Acts is at 11:29-30, where we are told that the church at Antioch sent a gift to the church in Judea. But the story of this offering does not suggest a common practice; indeed, quite the reverse, since Luke indicates that it was made under very extraordinary circumstances, as the consequence of a special prediction by a prophet named Agabus that "there would be a great famine over all the world." There is, of course, plenty of evidence in Paul's letters that the churches were expected to care for their poor. 2 Thess. 3:10 reflects the practice of assisting the needy from a common fund, as do Rom. 12:13 and passages in other letters also. But such passages cannot be cited to prove that there was a custom of sending money to *Jerusalem*.

Sometimes the tense of the word *remember* is cited as supporting this view. That tense is the present, the tense of continuous action. Ernest DeWitt Burton, surely an authority on such a point, writes, "The tense of μνημονεύωμεν, denoting continued action, indicates either that the course of action referred to is one which having already been begun is to be continued, or that there is distinctly in mind a practice (not a single instance) of it in the future."[4] Although Burton regards the former of the two meanings as "somewhat more probable," it is not clear that he does so on merely linguistic grounds. In any case, there is nothing whatever against the second. And that meaning is quite compatible with *c*, since the offering referred to in Corinthians and Romans was in process of being taken for two years at least, and Galatians, according to the usual dating, was written while it was in progress. Note also that 1 Cor. 16:2 directs, "On the first day of every week, each of you is to put something aside and save, as he may prosper, so that contributions need not be made when I come." In an allusion to such a collection, especially if the allusion is made while the collection is being taken, the present tense of *remember* seems almost required. Besides, is it not possible that Paul thought of the offering he was taking in the period of the Corinthian letters as the beginning of a practice?

---

[4]Ernest DeWitt Burton, *The Epistle to the Galatians*, International Critical Commentary (New York: Scribner's, 1920) 99.

Surely it is more probable that such was Paul's expectation after the of
fering should be taken than that it had been his practice before, in view of
the lack of any reference to it in his letters.

But if it should be decided that the present tense of *remember* looks—
be it ever so slightly—in the direction of a long-standing practice, the aor-
ist ἐσπούδασα ("I made haste") looks much more decisively in the direction of a single effort. "The verb," says Burton, "signifies not simply,
'to be willing,' nor, on the other hand, 'to do with eagerness,' but 'to make
diligent effort' to do a thing . . . ; cf. Jth. 13:1, 12, 'to make haste' to do
a thing. Apparently, therefore, it can not refer simply to the apostle's state
of mind, but either to a previous or subsequent activity on his part."[5] Note
that the reference is to *an activity* in particular, not to habitual activity. A
previous activity is ruled out as a possibility in this case by the fact, which
Burton notes, that the sentence here constitutes a stipulation in a contract,
"a qualification of an agreement." But such a qualification has no reality
if it has already been fulfilled. The "diligent effort" to which Paul refers,
then, must have taken place after the conference.

But when? Was it *(b)* an effort made and consummated, of which no
mention is made in Paul's letters or in any other source and of which all
trace has been lost; or was it *(c)* the effort of which we read so much in 1
and 2 Corinthians and Romans? In favor of *c* is the fact that Paul's references to the collection in these letters are such as to suggest neither a recognized custom nor an activity with a precedent but a unique undertaking.
Paul nowhere appeals to either a previous practice or a previous effort. In
writing to the Romans he not only has to inform them that an offering has
been taken, but he even has to explain why it is appropriate. No, every-
thing suggests that when the Jerusalem leaders proposed that the Gentile
churches in Paul's territory should "remember the poor," they were pro-
posing a new thing. Paul saw in this proposal a real opportunity to solve
the problem that had brought him to Jerusalem on this occasion, and he
immediately set out to raise as large a sum as possible. It was because the
offering had been undertaken under these circumstances and had this po-
tential meaning that Paul felt he must at all costs carry it himself to Jerusalem. He must dramatize and make fully effective its significance as a
peace offering on the part of the Gentile churches of which he was the head
and the symbol.

---

[5]Ibid., 99-100.

This connection between Gal. 2:10 and Rom. 15:25-32 is recognized by C. H. Dodd when he writes, "Paul does not add [to what he says in Rom. 15] that for him it was not only a moral obligation, but a contractual one, in view of his agreement with Peter, James and John.''[6] A. D. Nock states it equally clearly when, speaking of the period of the Corinthian letters, he writes, "The only bond between [Paul] and Jerusalem now is his collection of money for the benefit of the community there: he had promised that, and he would keep his part of the bargain.''[7] That Nock is identifying this collection with the special one referred to in the Corinthian letters and in Romans appears unmistakably when he writes in another connection, "From this center [Ephesus] Paul was to organize his collection for the benefit of the church at Jerusalem.''[8] And William Sanday and Arthur Headlam come close to implying the same connection when they allude to the offering as "the peace-offering of the Gentile Churches.''[9]

But what Dodd, Nock and many others apparently do not recognize is that to bring the offering of Corinthians-Romans into this kind of connection with Gal. 2:10 is to bring the visit to Jerusalem, which occurred "fourteen years later" (V in the outline), and the visit to convey the offering (VII) very close together. We cannot very well suppose that Paul got around to fulfilling his "contractual obligation" some ten years or so after the contract was made. The effort to raise the collection occupied perhaps as much as three years (cf. 2 Cor. 9:2), but surely not much longer. An interval of not more than four years is indicated between the "conference" and the "offering" visits almost as clearly and surely as though Paul had said again, "after three years. . . . ''

III

This means, of course, that when Paul made his visit to Jerusalem "fourteen years later" he had reached the zenith of his career. He had labored in Galatia and Asia, in Macedonia and Greece. It is true that he does not mention these various fields in Gal. 1:21, but there is not the slightest

---

[6]C. H. Dodd, *The Epistle of Paul to the Romans* (Moffatt Commentary; New York: Harper & Bros., 1932) 232.

[7]A. D. Nock, *St. Paul* (New York: Harper & Bros., 1938) 118-19.

[8]Ibid., 131.

[9]William Sanday and Arthur Headlam, *The Epistle to the Romans* (New York: Scribner's, 1911) 415.

reason why he should. He says, "Then I went into the regions of Syria and Cilicia"; but instead of going on to indicate where else he went, he returns his attention immediately to the point that alone was relevant: "I was still not known by sight to the churches of Christ in Judea." What was important in the argument was that he left Judea after his two-week visit; there was no occasion whatever for a description of all his subsequent activities. When he resumes, "Then after fourteen years I went up again to Jerusalem," he gives no indication of where he had been meanwhile, or of where he was when he began this journey. Johannes Weiss, although he is applying this point quite differently, makes it clearly when he writes, "Gal. 1:21 cannot be taken to mean that for the fourteen years, he worked *only* in Syria and Cilicia. The statement merely indicates the point from which his work at that time began, but does not in any way describe this work as a whole."[10] That Paul had reached Macedonia, Greece and Asia at the time of this "conference" visit is in some degree confirmed, however, by his statement that he took Titus with him, since Titus is not mentioned except in the Corinthian letters. If it should be objected that Barnabas went also, and that Barnabas, and Mark, broke with Paul much earlier in his career, we need only note that our only evidence that this break occurred earlier is in Acts. If Paul alludes to a break at all, he does so in Gal. 2:13, in what is apparently a sequel to the conference. (In Acts, too, the rupture with Barnabas occurs only after this conference.) If the conference, therefore, took place only a few years before the final visit, the disagreement with Barnabas cannot be dated earlier. We are bound also to notice the references to Barnabas in 1 Cor. 9:6 and to Barnabas and Mark in Col. 4:10. It is likely that these two men were known in both Corinth and Colossae.

If, then, we had only the letters of Paul, we should undoubtedly have something like the following understanding of the course of Paul's career after his conversion: He remained in the neighborhood of Damascus for three years or more. After a visit to Jerusalem to become acquainted with Cephas, he returned to Syria (probably to Antioch), then went on (probably soon afterward) to Cilicia. In the course of the next fourteen years he lived and worked in Galatia, Macedonia, Greece and Asia, and possibly elsewhere. He ran into increasing difficulty with conservative Jewish Christians, probably from Judea, and finally went to Jerusalem to talk with

---

[10]Johannes Weiss, *The History of Primitive Christianity* (New York: Wilson-Erickson, 1937) 1:204.

the leaders there about the growing rift. This conference ended, as we have seen, with their giving him the right hand of fellowship, but with the stipulation of aid for the poor. This aid Paul set about raising. In Romans we see him, the collection completed, ready to embark for Jerusalem to deliver it but apprehensive as to what will happen there.

Such is the story the letters tell, plainly and consistently. There is no remark or hint in them that is not entirely and naturally compatible with this story; and if we had only the letters, students of the life of Paul would accept it without question. And yet the story that for the most part they do actually accept is quite different from this; for, as a matter of fact, we are not in the position of having only the letters. We have the Acts of the Apostles as well, and instead of believing the story of the letters and using what we can of the Acts story (and there is much indeed that can be used), we have been inclined to believe the Acts story, because it is the more circumstantial, and to fit in, as well as possible, the bits from the letters. It is that procedure that is being challenged in these first chapters.

Let us now examine the story in Acts, noting especially the points where it differs from the story the letters, taken alone, seem to tell. If we find that in the points of difference recognizable interests of Luke-Acts are involved, we shall have gone far toward justifying our interpretation of the autobiographical material in the letters.[11]

----

[11] I should not want it to be supposed that I ever presumed the general idea of a three-Jerusalem-visit frame for Paul's career originated with me, although when I wrote the first article mentioned in the preface, I did not *know* that it did not. When the second article was written, however, I had learned that several scholars over the years had proposed such a frame, and I made due acknowledgment of that fact in the article. I believe it may be truly said, however, that none of these earlier writers, including the most recent of them, E. Barnikol, *Die drei Jerusalemreisen des Paulus* (Kiel: Muehau, 1929), came even close to my overall conception of proper method or to a chronology dependent on its use.

Chapter IV

The Evidence of Acts

It is obviously out of the question to reproduce the material from Acts relevant to our inquiry as was done from the letters of Paul. But we can make an outline of Paul's career as it appears there for comparison with the corresponding outline on page 34—using capital letters this time, rather than Roman numerals, to facilitate cross reference.

    A. Conversion on road to Damascus—Acts 9:1-8

    B. "Many days" in Damascus conferring with Ananias and preaching the new faith—9:10-25

    C. Return (first visit) to Jerusalem and first introduction to the apostles as a believer—9:26-27

    D. Preaching activity among believers and others in Jerusalem; departure for Cilicia; return to Antioch—9:28-30; 11:25-26

    E. Second visit to Jerusalem to bring relief in time of famine (12:25 being taken to refer to the return to Antioch "from Jerusalem," as against some manuscripts that read "to Jerusalem")—11:29-30; 12:25

    F. Activity in Syria, Cyprus, Galatia ("first missionary journey")—13-14

    G. Third visit to Jerusalem to the apostolic council—15:1-29

    H. Activity in Galatia, Macedonia, Greece and Asia ("second missionary journey")—15:36-18:21

    J. Fourth visit to Jerusalem, to greet the church—18:22

K. Activity in Syria, Galatia, Asia, Macedonia and Greece ("third missionary journey")—18:23-21:14
L. Fifth, and final, visit to Jerusalem—21:15

Fixing our attention on the "visits" to Jerusalem rather than on what happened in the intervals, we note at once a rough correspondence between C and III, on page 34, and between L and VII—that is, between the first and the last visits mentioned in Acts and the letters respectively. There are, to be sure, significant differences—we have already noted those between C and III (see pp. 22-23) and shall later have occasion to examine certain discrepancies between L and VII—but the correspondence here is unmistakable.

Still another point of correspondence can be established almost as surely, namely, between G and V—that is, between the second visit according to the letters and the third according to Acts. Again, there are significant differences: Paul describes a private, more or less informal, conference with "those who were of repute" about the question of the admission of uncircumcised Gentiles to the fellowship of the church; Luke describes an official council of apostles and elders in formal session, hearing the case and giving an authoritative decision. Paul asserts that the leaders "added nothing" to him except that he should "remember the poor"; Luke describes a compromise formula worked out by the apostles and elders governing the conditions under which the Gentiles might be received—a formula committed to writing in a letter that Paul and Barnabas are directed to convey to the several Gentile churches. But these differences are all such as we should expect from what we know of the purpose of Luke-Acts; that is, Luke's departures from what we must accept as the truer story told in Galatians are all fully explained by his interest in showing that the primitive church, Gentile and Jewish, was firmly united under the authority of the Twelve, and that Paul willingly followed their directions. In a word, there can be little doubt that the meeting in Jerusalem that Luke represents as an impressive apostolic council in Acts 15:1-29 is the same meeting that Paul has more accurately described in Gal. 2:1-10[1]

---

[1]The theory of some scholars that the visit of Gal. 2:1-10 (V) is identical with that of Acts 11:29-30; 12:25 (E) should not be dismissed too lightly. But for the fact that Barnabas is mentioned with Paul in both of these accounts, there is no point of correspondence between them, and it seems fair to say that no one would have thought of the possible identification had it not been for the exigencies of the usual Pauline chronology. It is precisely this chronology that is now under question (see also 49).

But if it is clear that Paul and Luke are speaking of the same meeting, it is almost as clear that they have different conceptions of when that meeting occurred. We have seen that on the basis of the letters alone we should certainly think of the conference visit as having taken place only three or four years at most before the final, or offering, visit. But Luke represents it as having occurred not long after Paul entered upon his career; the apostle had just returned to Antioch from his "first missionary journey" when the issue over the admission of Gentiles became acute, and he and Barnabas "were appointed to go up to Jerusalem to the apostles and the elders about this question" (Acts 15:2).

This problem of the *time* of the conference visit is really the crucial one in the study of the chronology of Paul's career. The principle governing the use of the sources we have adopted would require that we accept even a clear hint in the letters as having more value than the most explicit statement in Acts that contradicts it. We have seen in the preceding chapter that the conception of the conference as having come only a few years before the offering visit rests on more than a "clear hint" in the letters. But for fear that the demonstration may not have been fully convincing, or that some may not fully agree with the principle itself, let us look at some independent supporting arguments for the view that the conference did in fact take place not long before Paul's final visit to Jerusalem, and therefore near the end rather than at the beginning of his work as an apostle.

I

The first of these is the extreme difficulty of accommodating an interval of fourteen years—which, as we have seen, Paul vigorously, even solemnly, affirms—between the "acquaintance" visit and the "conference" visit. Can we find it credible that seventeen years (or at the very least fourteen) separated the conversion of Paul and his calling as an apostle (which every reference both in the letters and in Acts would lead us to suppose was closely connected with his conversion) from the work in western Asia Minor, Macedonia and Greece that is presupposed or described in the letters? None of his letters came out of this alleged interval, nor does Paul ever allude to any of his activities in it. Even Luke has little to say about it. It is, except for the "first missionary journey" at the very end of it, a silent period.

The difficulty of harmonizing this Pauline *interval* with the Lukan *position* of this conference visit appears greater when we take into account the most probable chronological limits of Paul's career as a whole. As to the time of his conversion, it is of course theoretically possible to place it in A.D. 30 or 31, or immediately after Jesus' crucifixion; but so early a date is on intrinsic ground quite unlikely, and it is highly doubtful that anyone would favor it if it were not that the exigencies of the Pauline chronology as a whole are felt to require it. When Paul's conversion took place, the new movement had spread to Damascus and not improbably to Antioch. As we have seen (pp. 21-22), it is likely that Paul's whole experience with Christianity, both as persecutor and as evangelist, lay outside of Palestine. Paul is a product of extra-Palestinian Christianity, and time must be allowed for the development of that phase of the movement. Thus, A.D. 34 is a more probable date for Paul's conversion than any earlier year.

As to the date of the final visit to Jerusalem, which marked the end of Paul's active career, we must depend only upon the Acts statement that this visit occurred some two years before Festus succeeded Felix as procurator of Judea. Although there is no corroborative evidence for this statement in the letters, there is no contradictory evidence, and there seems to be no adequate reason for distrusting it. The author of Luke-Acts describes at great length and with elaborate detail Paul's trials before Felix and his successor. If Paul's arrest did not occur somewhere in the neighborhood of the time when this change of administration took place, Luke-Acts is involved in an error which on any view of the date, authorship, or purpose of that work is almost incredible. We may assume, then, that Paul's final journey to Jerusalem came somewhat before Festus took Felix's place as procurator of Judea. But when was that? The evidence is somewhat confused, but on the whole points to A.D. 55.[2] To be sure, most scholars prefer a later date, but it is fair to say again that they do so, not on the basis of the evidence bearing on this particular point, considered independently and taken at face value, but, as in the other case, because of the requirements of the usually accepted chronology. Just as they have tended for this reason to push the date of the conversion back as far as possible, so they have been

---

[2]There are two pieces of evidence. One is the statement of Eusebius that the accession of Festus occurred in the second year of Nero, which would be 55-56 (*Chronicon*). The other is the statement of Josephus that Felix, after his term of office, was saved from disgrace by the intervention of Pallas (*Antiquities* XX. 8-9)—this statement taken with that of Tacitus that Pallas himself fell into disfavor in 55 (*Annals* XIII, 14-15). See also F. J. Foakes-Jackson and Kirsopp Lake, *Beginnings of Christianity,* pt. 1 (London: Macmillan & Co., 1933) 5:464-67.

inclined to press the time of the arrest forward as far as the evidence can be forced to allow. That it is considerations like these which in no small part determine the dating of both events will appear from an examination of the chronological schemes various modern students of Paul's life have adopted. Generally speaking, writers who take 55 or 56 as the date of Festus' accession put Paul's conversion in 30, 31 or 32. Writers who put the conversion as late as 35 place the accession of Festus in 57 or later. In each case it is apparently the supposed demands of the Pauline chronology as a whole that determine the scholar's opinion, rather than the evidence bearing directly upon the particular point.

Now if the more probable date for Festus's succession, A.D. 55, is adopted and Paul's final visit to Jerusalem is dated a year or so before, we are in the position of having to fit his career into the years separating 34 and 54. Within these years, seventeen silent years simply cannot be accommodated. For this reason, as we have seen, either we place the conversion as early as is theoretically possible, or we take advantage of some confusion in our sources to push the time of Festus's accession as late as possible, or both.

Another difficulty involved in the Acts position of the conference deserves to be mentioned before we take up an entirely different reason for accepting the position Paul's letters seem to give it. The apostle as we know him is very much concerned not to build upon another's foundation. He tells us that immediately after his conversion, instead of conferring with those who had been apostles before him, he went to Arabia, quite possibly to begin his preaching in a virgin field, quite possibly for some other reason. But it seems clear that Christianity had reached Antioch, and it is not unlikely that it had reached Tarsus. Would Paul have spent fourteen years in Syria and Cilicia? Would not this man who from the start insisted upon his independence of the disciples at Jerusalem—would he not have been equally insistent upon maintaining his independence of the disciples at Antioch? That he remained so long in another's field before entering upon a shorter stay in the field he was to make his own is on its face improbable. This improbability is enhanced by the absence of any indication of important surviving Pauline influence in Syria or Cilicia. When Ignatius early in the second century writes to the church at Ephesus, he does not claim Paul for Antioch; it is the Ephesians who are the "fellow-initiates" of the apostle.

For all of these reasons, and others we shall look into, it seems likely that although Luke in Acts 15:1-29 is referring to the same meeting that

Paul is describing in Gal. 2:1-10, he has placed it earlier in Paul's career than it belongs.

II

Without leaving this problem, let us now briefly consider the fourth visit to Jerusalem in the Acts scheme—J in our outline. We are bound to note at once the curious absence of any adequate occasion or motive for this visit. The whole trip back to Palestine from Paul's field seems to have no purpose except to fulfill the Lukan pattern of missionary journeys. Paul is in Corinth at Acts 18:17. He leaves for Syria, stopping on the way at Ephesus. He is urged to stay there for a while, but insists that he cannot do so. He takes his leave with the promise that he will return "if God wills." According to 18:22-23, "When he had landed at Caesarea, he went up [to Jerusalem[3]] and greeted the church, and then went down to Antioch. After spending some time there he departed and went from place to place through the region of Galatia and Phrygia, strengthening all the disciples." And so he returns to Ephesus, from which he has felt forced to tear himself away only three verses before! Why this elaborate journey? Is it merely an invention of Luke? In that case, why does he not invent a purpose also? Or did Luke's source tell him of this trip but not of its purpose? Or is it possible that *this* is the conference visit and that Luke, while keeping the visit for its value as bringing the "second missionary journey" to its end and as providing an additional point of contact of Paul with the church of Palestine and Syria, moves the actual *occasion* of it to the point earlier in Paul's career where the apostolic council visit now stands, in Acts 15:1-29? If the conference at Jerusalem over the Jewish issue stood in Acts 18 instead of in Acts 15, the major discrepancy between the letters and Acts would disappear and, along with it, any awkwardness in fitting the Pauline intervals with the Lukan incidents.

But why would Luke be interested in using the occasion of Paul's penultimate visit, which did occur, to explain an earlier visit, which did not? The answer is: Because he believed that the divisive issue between Greek and Jew in the primitive church was settled *early* and *finally*. He could not accept the fact that this issue was in its acutest phase at a time when Paul had done the major part of his work and was indeed approaching the end

---

[3]The Greek text does not include an explicit reference to Jerusalem, but the context strongly suggests that "the church" was there.

of his career. No reader of Acts 15:1-29 and Gal. 2:1-10 can ignore the important changes that Luke or some predecessor made in what must have been the original description of the conference in order to bring out the significance he found in it. If the conference took place as near the end of Paul's career as three or four years, its *position* also was subject to change in the interest of that same significance.

III

That visits G and J in the Acts scheme represent one visit and that this visit occurred in the J position, thus corresponding exactly with V in the letters scheme, appears the more likely in the light of certain facts about the Lukan stories of visits E and L, to which we have so far had no occasion to refer beyond pointing out the correspondence between L and VII.

As to the first of these visits, E—described in Acts 11:29-30 as having been made to bring relief to the Jerusalem church from Antioch—virtually everyone agrees that it could not have taken place. After all, Paul explicitly excludes the possibility of any visit between the acquaintance visit and the conference visit. Some scholars have sought to account for the discrepancy by arguing that the conference visit was also a relief visit—a visit with two purposes was mistakenly taken for two visits.[4] Some of these scholars have conceived of this double-purpose visit as happening at the point indicated by Acts 11:29 and others at the point indicated by Acts 15:1. But however the error is accounted for, the error itself is not denied; Luke is clearly mistaken in placing a visit of Paul to Jerusalem between the acquaintance and conference visits. But if there was an offering visit and if it did not occur *before* the conference, why is it not simplest to suppose that it occurred *after* the conference—especially as that is where Paul himself places such a visit?

That Luke moved the offering visit, properly placed as Paul's final one in the letters, to an earlier place in Paul's career is not mere conjecture. We have just noted the absence of any adequate purpose or occasion for the fourth visit in Acts (J—18:22) and have accounted for this lack by Luke's having utilized the original purpose of that visit for an earlier jour-

---

[4]The most influential suggestion of this kind was made by Eduard Schwartz, "Zur Chronologie des Paulus," *Nachrichten von der koeniglichen Gesellschaft der Wissenschaften zu Goettingen* (Berlin: Weidmann, 1907) 263ff.; reprinted in Eduard Schwartz, *Gesammelte Schriften* (Berlin: de Gruyter, 1963) 5:124ff.

ney to Jerusalem, which is said to have occurred soon after Paul's career began (G—15:1-29). In precisely the same way, the final visit (L—21:15) is not adequately motivated in the Acts narrative. Again in 20:3, as in 18:17, we find Paul at Corinth "about to set sail for Syria." No reason or motive for this journey is given. He goes through Macedonia and again comes to Ephesus, or at least to nearby Miletus. In an address to the elders of the Ephesian church, Paul lets us know that he expects to suffer death as a result of this journey, but in spite of such a prospect he does not think of turning back. Yet we are not told why it was so urgent for him to go on. The nearest Luke comes to explaining it is in the words, "For he was hastening to be at Jerusalem, if possible, on the day of Pentecost" (20:16). At Tyre and again at Caesarea, Paul is warned of the grave danger he is incurring by going to Jerusalem, but "he would not be persuaded." Still, Luke has given us no hint of why this desperately dangerous, almost certainly fatal visit must be made.

This time, however, we know from the letters not only that this visit was made but also why it was so urgently necessary; Paul was bringing a peace offering to the Jerusalem church (pp. 36-40). But Luke has not said one word about Paul's efforts to raise a fund for Judea, nor does he mention his having brought money until Acts 24:17. From that very casual reference we would hardly get the impression that the money he brought was an offering from Gentile to Jewish churches. Paul says before Felix, "Now after some years I came to bring to my nation alms and offerings," and verse 18 strongly suggests that the offering was brought to the temple itself. Thus it seems likely that Luke had some knowledge of the offering as a motive for the final journey, but he either misunderstood its nature and importance or deliberately refrained from emphasizing it, or even clearly mentioning it. That Luke had good sources, or a good source, for this journey appears not only in the fact that the "diary," a presumptive firsthand source, is used for parts of it, but also because Paul's movements just before he reached Corinth correspond exactly with what 1 and 2 Corinthians tell us. At Acts 19:21, while Paul is still in Ephesus, where he wrote 1 Corinthians, we read, "Now after these events Paul resolved in the Spirit to pass through Macedonia and Achaia and go to Jerusalem, saying, 'After I have been there, I must also see Rome.' " So accurate an account of Paul's intentions at this period indicates a good source. It seems unlikely that such a source would fail to mention the offering with which Paul and his associates were at this time so busily engaged. We are particularly aware of this omission in connection with Luke's account of the gathering at Philippi and Troas (20:4-7) of those who were to accompany Paul on this voyage to Jerusalem. 1 Cor. 16:3-4 prepares us to expect such a gathering, for its members are almost certainly the representatives of the several churches which have participated in the offering. The offering provides the only occasion of their taking this long journey, and Luke's source must have included this essential detail. And yet Luke allows only one brief, casual and somewhat misleading reference to the offering to get into his narrative—and this in a speech of Paul's delivered well after the narrative of the journey itself has been completed.

Why should this writer slight so important a fact? The obvious answer is the symbolic significance, which, as we have seen, made it so important. This offering was essentially a peace offering, but according to Luke-Acts there had been peace in the church for many years—indeed ever since the apostolic council, early in Paul's ministry. There was no occasion for a peace offering. In the very omission of the offering from Luke's story of this final journey we find, then, evidence that this effort was inseparably connected with the issue the Judaizers had raised. Since Luke's theory calls for the settlement of that issue years before, the offering, like the conference, must be relegated to an earlier period. Indeed, the offering is separated entirely from its original context. In Paul it is the sequel of the conference, both in time and in meaning; in Acts it precedes the conference and has no connection whatever with the Jewish question.[5]

IV

To sum up, we have in Paul's letters evidence that he made three trips to Jerusalem after his conversion, the purposes or occasions of which are indicated by the words *acquaintance, conference* and *offering*. We saw reason within the letters for believing that only these three visits were made. Acts, however, tells of five visits, but for only three of these are we told the occasions. The three occasions can again be indicated by the words *acquaintance, conference,* and *offering*. Is it not fair to suppose that these three visits correspond to the three visits with the same purposes that are mentioned in the letters? But Luke has modified their chronological po-

---

[5]Luke's interest in playing down the importance of this question is probably also to be seen in the account he gives of the cause of the break between Paul and Barnabas (cf. Gal. 2:13 and Acts 15:36-40).

sition. This is easily demonstrated in the case of the offering visit, since the offering visit in Acts could not have happened at the time assigned to it (11:29), and the evidence developed above seems to make it reasonably convincing in the case of the conference visit also.

If the conference visit occurred only a few years before the final visit, it is not necessary to suppose a silent period of from fourteen to seventeen years, or even more, before Paul was launched on the work with which alone either Acts or his letters are concerned, and it is not necessary to crowd that work into a period too short for it. It was from Ephesus or Corinth, not from Antioch, that Paul made his trip to Jerusalem ''after fourteen years.''

The principal reasons for such a view are derived from the letters and have been discussed in chapter 3. This chapter has been concerned, not with proving the hypothesis, but with showing that a critical examination of Luke-Acts from the point of view of this hypothesis yields results that at certain points strikingly confirm the hypothesis itself.

One of the principal advantages of this way of conceiving of Paul's career is that it makes possible a more rational reconstruction of the course of Paul's relations with the Judaizers than is otherwise possible. According to the conventional (Acts) chronology, the issue with them is acutely raised at several intervals: near the beginning of Paul's work, before the ''council''; when Galatians was written, probably many years later; and at the time of the offering, as we see from Rom. 15:31. The proposed scheme, on the other hand, brings Paul's conference with the leaders at Jerusalem about the status of the Gentile churches into the years when his letters, especially Galatians and Romans, reflect concern with that same issue, and when the collection, Paul's decision to take it himself to Jerusalem and his final arrest there indicate its great and growing importance.[6]

---

[6]This significance of the proposed chronology is explored by Donald M. Riddle, *Paul, Man of Conflict* (New York and Nashville: Abingdon, 1940).

Chapter V

□———————————□

A Biographical Sketch

In the preceding chapters of this book I have attempted to do three things: First, to present, illustrate, and defend the proper method of using the letters of Paul and the book of Acts in recovering the life of Paul; second, to demonstrate that one—and, as far as the active career of the apostle is concerned, the most important—result of the application of this method is the perception that Paul made only three visits to Jerusalem after his conversion (not five, as the Acts narrative avers); and, third, to establish the probability of the dates 34 and 54 (or dates in their close neighborhood) for the beginning and the end, respectively, of Paul's career as a Christian evangelist.

We are now in position to attempt a fuller account of Paul's life and to move toward a more detailed chronology of it.

I

We can only guess at the year of Paul's birth. Our only data for its determination are the facts that Paul was a grown man at the time of his conversion to Christianity and that he was a still vigorously active man at the time when Festus succeeded to the procuratorship of Judea. But whether the conversion be dated in A.D. 34 or earlier and Festus's accession in A.D. 55 or later, Paul obviously might have been born at any time within a decade of the beginning of our era, that is, between 10 B.C. and A.D. 10. According to the usual text of Philem. 9, Paul calls himself an "old man" (πρεσβύτης), but it is likely that his term was *ambassador* (πρεσβευτής), since this fits the context perfectly and is strongly suggested by Eph. 6:20, where he is described as "an ambassador in chains." Also, it is uncertain when Philemon was written. These doubts preclude our using that remark as a significant datum. We are not in better position for tracing the incidents of Paul's life in the period that lies between his birth and those later events with which his letters put us in touch. We have seen that there is no reason to distrust the Acts tradition that he was born in Tarsus, but Paul's own statements clearly indicate that he was in Damascus at the time of his conversion and, almost as clearly, that he had previously been a persecutor of the church in that same city and district. But as to how it happened that he was there or as to any of the earlier turns or fortunes of his career he tells us nothing.

We do not know the extent or character of his education. We can assume that since he was of a devout Jewish home, he received the elementary education at the synagogue school which every Jewish boy would receive in any locality where any considerable Jewish colony was found. This would be true of Tarsus or, for that matter, of Damascus. It is probable also that Paul had an early and active interest in rabbinical theology. One does not need to assume, however, that he was preparing for the rabbinate. He nowhere claims to have been expert in the law, only zealous of carrying it out. As to the suggestion sometimes made that Paul attended one of the universities, such as that of Tarsus, one can only say that it is most unlikely. Paul shows as little sign of being learned in the Hellenistic as in the Jewish sense. Except for a citing of what Moffatt calls a "popular tag" from Menander in 1 Cor. 15:33, Paul never quotes from the Greek philosophers and poets nor so much as refers to them. It is Luke (Acts 17:28) and the writer of the Pastoral epistles (Tit. 1:12) who attribute such references to Paul, and such vague reminiscences of philosophical language as may be found in his writings, as possibly some echoes of Aristotle in Rom. 2:14-15, can be fully accounted for by his having heard, as he could hardly have avoided, the popular Stoic-Cynic preachers who taught philosophy to any who would listen in the markets and streets of any large Hellenistic city. From them also Paul derived the vigorous conversational, question-and-answer style, the so-called diatribe, which is almost as characteristic of his letters as of the discourses of Epictetus. That Paul was a man of active, alert mind and great intellectual capacity, that he had had some contact with Greek philosophy and that he had some knowledge of rabbinical theology must be fully granted. But there is no evidence of advanced formal training either in Hellenistic wisdom or in scribal learning.

We do not know his vocation before he became an apostle. Jewish boys of every class normally learned some trade. According to Acts, Paul had acquired the skill of a tentmaker, or perhaps a weaver (the proper translation of the Greek term is uncertain). Since he alludes several times to his working with his hands, it is to be presumed that he supported himself by this trade in his later years. But it is unlikely that a man of his gifts had always been actively, or at any rate fully, occupied with such a trade. Perhaps his family had been able to support him; perhaps he had been in business. These are the merest guesses. We only know that he entered, a grown man, upon the stage of history at Damascus as a determined persecutor of a new movement within Judaism that seemed to him and to many Jews to threaten that whole distinctive way of life upon which the Jew depended for the survival of the nation.[1] We have already examined the reasons for believing that Paul's conversion, which suddenly turned the persecutor into the apostle, should be dated not earlier that A.D. 34.[2] Paul tells us that immediately after this transforming ex-

---

[1]The specific grounds for Paul's persecuting the new movement are not made clear in any source. It is unlikely that the mere fact of Jesus' being called Messiah will explain Paul's bitter hostility—unless one accepts the brilliant but overbold suggestion of Hugh J. Schonfield, *The Jew of Tarsus: An Unorthodox Portrait of Paul* (New York: Macmillan, 1947) that Paul entertained at this time the secret belief that he himself had been designated the Messiah, a belief that was transmuted after "Damascus" into his sense of being in a unique way "the apostle to the Gentiles." Jews were tolerant in the field of belief; we know of other "Messiahs" whose followers were not persecuted. Presumably the Jewish believers in Jesus as Messiah were *acting* in un-Jewish ways—for example, disregarding the food and Sabbath laws or having intimate intercourse with Gentiles, perhaps even admitting the latter to the full fellowship of the church.

[2]I have spoken of Paul's conversion as turning the persecutor into the apostle—the moment of his becoming a Christian believer being the same as that of his apostleship's beginning. I speak to the same effect throughout this book, and it is in this way, so far as I know, that Gal. 1:15 has always been understood. Very recently, however, I have read in manuscript an essay by J. Peter Bercovitz in which it is argued that Paul was already a confessed follower of the Christian "way" when the revelation, which qualified him to be an apostle, occurred. This understanding of Gal. 1:15, Bercovitz maintains, would be the generally adopted one if we were not looking through "Acts-colored glasses." Paul was already one of the "called" when the Damascus event happened. Because of what seem to be the implications of the immediately preceding verses (11-14), I am not ready, at least as yet, to accept his conclusion, but neither can I confidently reject it. (But

perience he went to Arabia, the country just to the east and south of Syria. The border was close to Damascus; indeed, it has sometimes been held that in or about this period Damascus belonged to Arabia rather than to Syria. We do not know where Paul went in Arabia or why. The only reasons it is supposed that he went for solitude and meditation are, first, that he says he "did not confer with flesh and blood" and, second, that the word "Arabia" means to us deserts and the solitary life. The second of these reasons has no force at all, and the first hardly more. There were cities in Arabia, and there is no reason to suppose Paul did not visit one of them. Possibly, he had hopes of a successful preaching mission in that area. If so, we may be sure, in the absence of any further reference to it in the letters or elsewhere, that his hopes were disappointed. The hostile pursuit of him by Aretas (2 Cor. 11:32-33) may point to the same fact. But these are the merest guesses. We simply do not know either the where or the why of this Arabian trip. We do know that he returned directly to Damascus, that after three years he made his first visit to Jerusalem, and that a period of fourteen years separated this visit from the second.

We thus arrive at a roughly seventeen-year interval between his conversion and appointment as an apostle—for those were closely associated in time, if not absolutely concurrent—and the second, the so-called conference, visit. We cannot be sure of the seventeen years as an exact figure because the ἔπειτα in 1:18 and 2:1 may mean "after three [or fourteen] years" or "in the third [or fourteenth] year" and also because we cannot know whether in 1:18 the term refers to the conversion experience or to Paul's return from Arabia to Damascus. Still, since it appears likely that his stay in Arabia was relatively brief, our estimate of seventeen years can with a fair degree of certainty be regarded as correct—approximately correct at least. Perhaps to say sixteen to seventeen years would be safer.

II.

But where and how were these years spent? We know that he spent the first few of them in Damascus (and Arabia), and, from Gal. 1:21, that after

---

see 102-103 below.) As far as the chronology of Paul's life is concerned, the question is not very important since the interval between the conversion and the consciousness of apostleship must in any case have been short. As regards the chronology of his *apostolic career*, it obviously has no relevance at all. The essay appears in volume 5 of the *Proceedings of the Eastern Great Lakes and Midwest Biblical Societies*, 28-38, under the title, "Kalein ('To Call') in Gal. 1:15: Evidence That Paul Was Already a Believer When Christ Appeared to Him."

a very brief visit in Jerusalem he went to Syria and Cilicia. But the absolute absence of references in his letters to churches established by him in these areas or to his having any continuing influence or authority there, taken together with his strong assertion in Rom. 15:20 that he has been faithful in not building on foundations laid by others, would suggest that any labors of his in these regions were of relatively short duration. What happened then? What happened after his brief stay in Cilicia? I believe that *if we had only the letters as sources* (and we are assuming for the moment that such were the case), the consensus of scholarly opinion would be that his course continued in a westerly direction and, since he can speak later of his preaching in Macedonia as being "in the beginning of the Gospel" (Phil. 4:15), that after no long period he reached that province. This consensus, however, although supported by no explicit statement in the letters, would rest not only, or even chiefly, on the Philippians passage. It would rest also on the impression the letters give of the character of the man himself and of the nature of his calling. With the very beginning of his experience as a Christian came the assurance that he was called to preach the gospel to the nations, which for Paul would have meant the Mediterranean world. His resolution on such a mission, with Europe as the immediate goal, would have been taken early. It may indeed have been part of the motivation for his first visit to Jerusalem to talk with Peter and James (Gal. 1:18). He may well have felt that he should not embark on it without some contact and, he might hope, some common understanding with the earlier apostles. If he did, in fact, make his decision so early, his departure from Jerusalem for Syria and Cilicia was the beginning of its execution.

As to his route from Cilicia to Macedonia or as to events on the way, the letters alone would give us no clue. But his most direct route would have been through or near the cities of Iconium, Derbe, Lystra, Antioch and perhaps other places in southern Galatia, and it would not have been unreasonable to suspect that the gospel was planted there in the course of Paul's journey across Asia Minor early in his ministry. All of these conclusions as to probabilities would have been based only on what the letters suggest. It may be noted, however, that Acts 15:41-16:12 tells us that Paul reached Macedonia by way of Syria and Cilicia and the cities of southern Galatia, and it may not be irrelevant in this connection to observe that it is toward the end of this account of Paul's journey from Cilicia to Philippi that the so-called "diary" makes its first appearance.

"But," a critic may say, "what about the 'first missionary journey' (Acts 13-14)? Time for it must surely be allowed before this departure westward from Cilicia." My answer to this question is implicit in my rejection of the whole "missionary journey" scheme.[3] But if a more explicit and specific answer is asked for, I should say that the "first missionary journey" did not occur at all—*that is, as a part of Paul's career*. That there was an Antiochene mission I should not be disposed to question, although whether it went so far beyond Cyprus as to include the cities of southern Galatia can plausibly be doubted for reasons I shall shortly give. But whatever the extent of this possible, even probable, mission, I should be inclined to deny that Paul had any connection with it. I would feel serious doubt about such a connection simply for the same reason I would question anything in Acts involving Paul that is not explicitly or by clear implication indicated also in the letters, and in this case the letters are completely silent. But my doubting moves toward denying because the silence does not stand alone. Other considerations point in the same direction.

Up to this point (that is, Acts 13-14) every statement of Acts about Paul can be demonstrated to be either inaccurate or highly improbable. Paul is mentioned first in Acts 7:58 as consenting to the murder of Stephen and in 8:1-3 as participating in the persecution of the church in Jerusalem that followed. But Paul clearly denies in Gal. 1:22 that either of these statements is true. Luke's next mention of Paul is in Acts 9:1-30, which in its entirety is irreconcilable with Paul's Galatians account of his Damascus experience and its aftermath. Barnabas's finding Paul in Tarsus and bringing him to Antioch (11:25-26) is not, it is true, provably false, but in the context it is improbable. These actions seem little more than the necessary prelude to the involving of Paul in an offering visit to Jerusalem (11:27-30), but we know from an implicit denial in the letters that if such a visit occurred at all, Paul had no part in it. And the same denial can be made of the truth, as regards Paul, of 12:25, whether the disputed reading is ἐξ or εἰς. Thus we are brought to chapters 13 and 14. But if all the Acts statements about Paul up to this point are either demonstrably inaccurate or of extremely doubtful accuracy (and the same can be said of the following chapter, 15:1-35), why should we believe without any supporting evidence the statements in these chapters?

Moreover, in view of all the letters reveal of Paul and his sense of calling—"an apostle not from men or through men"—can we really see him

---

[3]See above, 25-26.

going forth ordained and instructed by the elders at Antioch on a mission as Barnabas's subordinate? I find it impossible to do so. I do not doubt that some ancient and true traditions lie buried in Acts 13-14, some of them associated with Cyprus and others with the Galatian cities. But I believe I have given good reasons for our questioning, to say the least, Paul's being associated with Barnabas in either locality. Perhaps traditions about Barnabas in Cyprus and Paul in southern Galatia have been fused into a single story by the final author of Luke-Acts or by one of his sources. It is my opinion that, so far as Paul is concerned, that author had only sparse, scattered traditions and his own historical imagination to depend on up to the point represented by Acts. 15:40. Only from that point on did he have sufficient source material for anything like a consecutive account of Paul's travels, possibly because it was at that point that Paul's travels really began. I see Acts 15:41 as answering to Gal. 1:21.

Whatever one's estimate of the argument I have been making in the last several paragraphs, I believe there may be general agreement that it is improbable that such cities as Iconium and Antioch, Hellenistic cities located in the very heart of southern Asia Minor, were not reached by the gospel fairly early. I concede readily that this fact cannot be proved. Conceivably, Christianity was planted in the remote cities of ethnic Galatia to the north, as well as in the Greek peninsula and even Asia before it was brought to these cities. But is this intrinsically likely? As long as we trust Acts 13-14, this question does not arise and therefore it has rarely, if ever, been considered. But if we distrust these chapters and still believe the gospel reached these southern Galatian cities quite early, is it not reasonable to suspect that it reached them while Paul was making his way from Syria and Cilicia to Macedonia?

One may further ask whether, if this is true, it is not probable—indeed, more than probable—that the churches established in those cities were among the "churches of Galatia" which were instructed about the collection for Jerusalem (1 Cor. 16:1) some years afterward and were addressed under that same name in his letter later still. I say "included among" for it is quite incredible that if in cities Luke describes as situated in Pisidia and Lycaonia, but which could equally aptly be described as located in Galatia—if in these cities a vital beginning was made for the gospel, whether by Paul alone or by Barnabas and Paul—it is incredible that in a decade it would not have reached northward, possibly even as far as ethnic Galatia. But if this is true and Paul has in this later time occasion to refer

to, or to address, the whole group of congregations, how shall he do so
except as "the churches of Galatia" (Gal. 1:2)? (Witness Paul's references to the "churches of Asia" [1 Cor. 16:19]. Actually, all of his geo-
graphical references, except to cities, are in terms of the Roman provincial
system of his day.)

But if one takes this position and recognizes that these southern Galatian churches were a part—indeed, probably the center—of Galatian
Christianity as Ephesus was of the movement in Asia, then one must give
up any idea not only that Paul participated in the "first missionary journey," but also that this "journey" (now seen as a journey of Barnabas and
Mark) extended as far as the cities of Antioch, Iconium and the rest. The
Epistle to the Galatians makes indubitable the fact that it was *Paul* (not Paul
and Barnabas) who first brought the gospel to the churches being addressed. The letter, throughout and in the most emphatic way, identifies
them as *his* churches. *He* founded them; *he* has nurtured them; *he* has made
two visits to them (4:13). And if it is asked, *"When* did he found them and
when did he visit them a second time?"*, the natural answer is that he
founded them on his way from Syria and Cilicia to Macedonia (Gal. 1:21–
Acts 15:41 [?]), and he visited them a second time on his way back to
Ephesus after the conference (Gal. 2:1-10) seeking their cooperation in the
collection he had just now undertaken (1 Cor. 16:1).

The fact that this first visit to the cities of Galatia was connected in some
way with bodily illness or disability (Gal. 4:13) throws little, if any, light
on where they were located, whether north or south. Nevertheless, it would
seem much more likely that the illness was the occasion of an interrupting
of a planned itinerary than that it was a reason for the itinerary itself. And
if this is true, surely the south Galatian cities come nearer to being indicated than, say, Pessinus to the north. Galatians 4:13 may well mean that
in his haste to reach Macedonia he might have passed south Galatia by if
illness or disability had not stopped him. It would appear less probable that
he could have gone to north Galatia without having intended to go there.
This is, needless to say, little more than guessing. We simply cannot know.
But certainly this reference does not require the "north Galatia hypothesis." Neither does any other reference ("so quickly" [Gal. 1:6], "O fool-
ish Galatians" [3:1], or any other) require it. I forbear traversing familiar
ground in justifying this denial.

However questionable some, or all, of my proposal may be as to Paul's
route from Syria and Cilicia to Macedonia (and no proposal can be de-

monstrably true), once he reached that province, there can be no doubt as to the direction of his next moves—from Philippi, to Thessalonica, to Athens and eventually to Corinth. This movement southward 1 Thessalonians and Philippians make altogether clear and certain, and the fact that the Acts story agrees in this respect adds nothing to our assurance. But as to how long he stayed in these cities we have no definite indication. One would gather that he may have remained in Philippi and Thessalonica a year at least—perhaps several years in both of the Macedonian cities—and, from silences, that he spent a shorter time in Athens. These, again, are hardly more than guesses, as anyone's estimates must be. Such also is any setting of time limits to his first stay in Corinth. But the reader of the Corinthian letters is likely to gain the impression that it was a more extended one—a real *residence* as contrasted with later *visits*.

But it certainly would not have lasted indefinitely long, or indeed longer than necessary, for Paul could not have forgotten that Ephesus, hitherto unevangelized, had been left in his wake, and he would have wanted to see the gospel established there before he proceeded, as he intended, to Italy and beyond. There are indications in the letters (Corinthians, Colossians, Philemon) that his stay in Ephesus was a prolonged one even as compared with that in Corinth. This conclusion receives some confirmation from Acts (compare 18:11 and 19:10). And such sources as Ignatius's letter to the Ephesians and the anti-Marcionite prologues suggest that Paul was later thought of as residing longer in Ephesus than in any other city. It is probable that the conference journey to Jerusalem began there, and it is plausible to surmise that it was on his way back to Ephesus that his promised visit to the churches of the Lycus valley (Philem. 22), as also his second visit to Galatia, occurred (compare Acts 18:23). The imprisonment in Ephesus for which Colossians, Philemon and Philippians offer some evidence could have occurred before the conference (2 Cor 1:8-9 does not necessarily imply an imprisonment). Although 1 Corinthians and 2 Corinthians (certainly for the greater part) were obviously written after the conference, one cannot exclude the possibility that the earlier letter, referred to in 1 Cor. 5:9, belonged to the prior period, once the possibility of such a period is acknowledged.

We have thus far been dealing with the seventeen-year period between the conversion and the Jerusalem conference. As to the following interval, that between the conference visit and the third and presumably final one, enough has been said in chapter 3 to justify the conviction that it was relatively brief. The interval between Paul's undertaking to make the collection for the Jerusalem church and its delivery could not have been long. On the other hand, time must be allowed for one, perhaps two, visits to Corinth before the final one and for some exchange of correspondence. The crisis in Galatia that called forth Paul's impassioned letter may also have occurred in this period, although it is my own inclination to date that letter later.[4] On the whole, I would propose an interval of four years or, let us say, of three or four years between the second (or conference) visit and Paul's departure from Corinth on the third.

I must repeat what has been said a number of times that the time estimates made in this chapter are for the greater part very tentative. The only interval of which we can be virtually sure is the thirteen to fourteen years separating Paul's first Jerusalem visit from the second. The interval of approximately three years between his conversion and the first visit can be almost as certain. We can thus be fairly well assured of a roughly seventeen-year period between his conversion and the conference visit. And now I have proposed an additional three or four years before his departure on his last visit to Jerusalem—a total of twenty or twenty-one years between his conversion and the last glimpse the letters give us of him.

Before raising the question of what happened to Paul after this final departure from Corinth and the even more vexing question of absolute dating, it may be useful to make a schedule of relative times in accordance with the suggestions I have ventured to make.

PAUL'S CAREER	DATE
a. Conversion and Call to Apostleship x	
Residence in Damascus with journey to Arabia	
and a stay of uncertain but probably short length there.	
b. First Jerusalem Visit .... x + 3	
Syria, Cilicia, Southern Galatia.	

---

[4]See Knox, "Galatians, Letter to the," *The Interpreter's Dictionary of the Bible* (New York and Nashville: Abingdon, 1962) 2:338-43. See also H. L. Ramsey, "The Place of Galatians in the Career of Paul" (Ph.D. diss., Columbia University, 1960; Ann Arbor: University Microfilms, 1961). This work is worthy of far more attention than it has received. Note the judgment of it, and the use of it, by Gerd Luedemann, *Paul, Apostle to the Gentiles,* trans. F. S. Jones (Philadelphia; Fortress, 1984) esp. 1:29 n3.

c. Arrival in Macedonia .... x + 6
Residence in Philippi, Thessalonica.
Work in Macedonia.
Stay, probably short, in Athens.
d. Arrival in Corinth .... x + 9
Residence there with work in Achaia.
e. Arrival in Ephesus .... x + 12
Prolonged residence there, marked by various missions,
possibly by an imprisonment, and, most important, by his
f. Second Jerusalem Visit (Conference) .... x + 17
Activity based in Ephesus concerned chiefly with Collection
and involving one or more visits to Corinth.
g. Departure from Ephesus for Corinth
to complete Collection .... x + 20
h. Departure from Corinth on Third Visit to Jerusalem
to deliver Collection .... x + 20-21

III

This final journey to Jerusalem (h in the foregoing schedule) is spoken of by Paul only in prospect. But his letters give ample grounds for some fairly confident expectations about it, notably, that he will not go alone but will be accompanied by delegates from the churches that have participated in the collection effort. Gerd Luedemann's surmise that, since only Macedonia and Achaia are mentioned in Rom. 15:26, the effort in Galatia had failed, and that therefore no Galatian representatives were included in the company, becomes less plausible when we note that Asia also is not mentioned in that passage. Yet, can there be any question but that the Asian churches, particularly the church at Ephesus, were involved? To be sure, Luedemann thinks there is such a question and, consistent with his opinion about the Galatians, holds that the Ephesians, too, "did not organize a collection because the apostle could not (any longer?) gain a foothold there."[5] He cited 1 Cor. 15:32 and 2 Cor. 1:8 in this connection. I must differ from him at this point. There would be no disagreement between us, I feel sure, as to the fact that Paul worked (himself and through his aides) for a considerable period in Ephesus and in other parts of Asia (witness Colossae, Laodicea and Hierapolis; no doubt there were other cities) and that his re-

---

[5]*Paul, Apostle to the Gentiles,* 1:86.

lations with these churches were warm and close, even in the very period when the collection effort was being made (1 Cor. 16:19). And there is nothing to indicate that they had altered for the worse when he left Ephesus finally (so far as we know) for Troas, Macedonia and Corinth. It is not at all necessary to understand the crisis suffered there (2 Cor. 1:8-9) as involving an alienation from the Ephesian church or even that the occasion of the suffering had any connection with that church at all. Besides, from this trouble, whatever it was, Paul can say that he was delivered. He did fight wild beasts in Ephesus, whatever that means, but again there is no hint that any alienation from the Ephesian church was entailed. Indeed, he speaks of this experience in the very letter in which cordial relations with that church are unmistakably reflected (1 Cor. 16:19). I have said in discussions of the date of Galatians that it is difficult to understand Paul's being able to speak so complacently in Romans 15 about his work from Jerusalem to Illyricum if he was at that very time in a state of alienation from the churches of Galatia;[6] but that difficulty is enormously increased if Asia, too, was estranged. In considering the fact of Paul's silence about the collection in Asia, it may be well to reflect that we should know little about Paul's effort in Macedonia and Achaia if it were not for the Corinthian letters. But there *is* no letter to the Ephesians! And may not this fact itself point to his having his base or headquarters there? In addition to such considerations as these in support of the view that Paul's relations with Ephesus were close and cordial, I find impressive evidences of a tradition to that effect of which I have made earlier mention in this chapter.

Luedemann makes the point that there was Christianity in Ephesus before Paul began his work there.[7] But as compared with the question of Paul's relations with the Ephesian church and other churches of Asia, especially in the period of the collection, the question of whether he can be spoken of as the founder of these churches is unimportant. Paul says nothing to indicate that he was not, and his affirmation in Romans that he had sought always not to build on others' foundations (Rom. 15:20; cf. 2 Cor. 10:15-16 and 1 Cor. 3:10-15) should lead us to conclude that he at least was able sincerely to feel that he had not done so in this case. It is true that Acts speaks of the earlier presence in Ephesus of a John the Baptist movement

---

[6]"Galatians, Letter to the," IDB 2:342.

[7]*Paul, Apostle to the Gentiles,* 1:146 and n16.

and represents Prisca and Aquila, through the conversion of Apollos to the new Way, as having formed a brotherhood, although apparently it was still attached to the synagogue. Paul on his return from a journey is said to have made additional converts from among these disciples of John. Eventually these Christians were forced to separate themselves from the synagogue. This whole story in Acts (18:18-19:9) is confused, obviously represents a fusion of probably conflicting traditions, and can hardly be understood, much less trusted. There is evidence in 1 Cor. 16:19 and (for what it may be worth) in Rom. 16:3 of Paul's close association with Prisca and Aquila, and any work they may have done in Ephesus before Paul's arrival would have been regarded by both him and them as being basically Paul's, just as the work of Epaphras in Laodicea and Colossae was. But, as I have said, I cannot see this whole question, actually unanswerable in detail or with assurance, of the remote origins of Christianity in Ephesus as bearing in any significant way on the matter of the obligation of the Ephesian church to participate in the offering or of its willingness to do so. It may be worth noting that the group that, according to the "we-source," accompanied Paul to Jerusalem to deliver the offering included the Asians Tychicus and Trophimus, as well as the Derbean (?) Gaius (Acts 20:4).

So, on the whole, despite the problem Rom. 15:26 presents, I am inclined to adhere to my view that both Galatia and Asia were participants in the collection effort and that Paul was able to present the offering to "the saints" as a gesture of gratitude and loyalty, not on the part of some of his churches only, but on the part of them all.

Besides the testimony the letters bear to the fact of the "final" journey to Jerusalem and to the fact that Paul was accompanied by representatives of these churches, they provide us with one other important fact, as was pointed out in chapter 3. They let us know that Paul was expecting to encounter serious threats to his liberty and even his life at the end of the journey. That he knew of and feared these threats, Rom. 15:30-32 says clearly, even eloquently; and once we are made aware of them, we can hardly fail to see a hint of them in 1 Cor. 16:3-4. There we learn that Paul wanted to avoid this journey. Undoubtedly, one reason for this wish was his impatience to be off to Rome and regions farther westward. But, in the light of Rom. 15:30ff., can we doubt that another and probably even more poignant reason was his fear of dangerous developments in Jerusalem that might not only further delay his going to Rome, but conceivably prevent it altogether? But so important did he regard the offering in healing the threatened breach in the church that he finally reluctantly decided that he could not simply delegate the delivery of it to others; he had to go to Jerusalem himself. Thus the letters alone would prepare us to learn of his arrest there. But for an actual account of both the journey and its sequel our only source is Acts, and the necessary cautions apply.

Luke devotes a very substantial part of his second volume to this journey and its aftermath, from 20:3 to 28:30—almost a third of the entire book and more than one-half of that part of the book in which Paul is the dominant figure. How much confidence can we have in the truth of these final chapters? Looked at from this point of view they constitute a very mixed bag. Luke begins with Paul in Corinth—a good beginning, as we have seen. The route by way of Macedonia and Troas is not at all improbable. Paul's being joined there by persons from Macedonia, Derbe (Galatia?) and Asia is entirely in line with Paul's allusion to his having companions on his journey. I see no reason to question the itinerary from Troas to Jerusalem, by way of Tyre and Caesarea. The fact that this part of the narrative has its source in the mysterious travel diary to some degree confirms its truth.

But there are many reasons to question the accuracy of much of the following narrative. To be sure, the fact that conflict arose involving Jewish enemies of Paul and eventually the Roman authorities is not at all unexpected in view of what Paul himself has told us of his fears, and the fact of his eventual arrest is not surprising. But under what conditions and for what reason the authorities took this action we cannot, in light of what we know of Luke's interests and method, avoid being more doubtful. A great deal of space is devoted to Paul's speeches, most of them his own apologetic explanations of his actions—speeches that deserve no more credence than all the speeches previously attributed to him. And, as has been suggested earlier in these pages, our knowledge of Luke is bound to make us suspicious that the creator of the speeches had some part in creating the occasions for them.[8] He tells of Paul's eloquent addresses before Felix, Festus and Agrippa (not to mention earlier speeches to the people and the Sanhedrin), and of the favorable impression Paul made on all three. How fortunate that his arrest took place at such a propitious time! Could Paul— or Luke—have wished for a happier juncture of circumstances and personages? Thus grave doubt is thrown on the only chronological datum in

---

[8]See above, 27.

the account—namely, that Paul's arrest took place not long before Festus succeeded Felix as Procurator of Judea.

IV

Before turning directly to some attempt at absolute dating, I should like to point out the unimportance of such dating as compared with the task of determining the length of Paul's career as an apostle and the course of events within it. For the understanding of Paul it matters little, if at all, just when, in terms of calendar years, his work began or just when it ended. What matters is what happened in it—the order of events and the intervals between them. In other words, what I called a "schedule of relative times," which I suggested earlier, is far more important than the schedule of absolute dates I shall later propose—far more important and, I should say, considerably less uncertain. But this statement of mine would be incomplete without my making some such proposal, so that with this understanding of its comparative unimportance, and with very great tentativeness, I shall proceed.

We may begin by observing that on this matter Paul himself gives us very little help. Indeed, his only reference to a possibly datable event is found in 2 Cor. 11:32-33, where he tells us that when he left Damascus on some unidentified occasion: "The governor under King Aretas guarded the city of Damascus in order to seize me, but I was let down in a basket through a window in the wall and escaped his hand." Acts 9:23-25 alludes to this same incident. Since Paul leaves us to suppose that he did not go back to Damascus after leaving it for his first Jerusalem visit, it is probable that in the 2 Corinthians passage he is alluding to that same departure. It could not have occurred later than A.D. 40, when Aretas's reign in Arabia (or Nabatea) ended. Robert Jewett believes he has established as quite solidly assured a date within the last two years of Aretas's regime, that is, in A.D. 37-39;[9] but I do not think that many scholars would share his assurance. To say this is to say that Paul's letters themselves, except within broad limits, provide us with no clue as to the date of his conversion. We can be quite certain, needless to say, that it occurred after Jesus' crucifixion and, with great probability because of the Aretas reference, not later than A.D. 37 (that is, A.D. 40 less the three years of Gal. 1:18). But as to how long after the crucifixion it took place is a very open question, and even the date of the crucifixion itself is subject to dispute, estimates ranging from A.D.

---

[9]Robert Jewett, *A Chronology of Paul's life* (Philadelphia: Fortress, 1979) 30-33.

27 to 33. The conversion, then, may conceivably have occurred in any year between, say, A.D. 32 and 37.

If it is impossible for us to know with certainty the date of the *beginning* of the twenty to twenty-one-year period we are concerned with, it is natural to ask, "Can we succeed any better in establishing the year in which it *ended*?" Obviously, if the conversion can be dated between A.D. 32 and 37 and if our estimate of a twenty to twenty-one-year interval between that event and his last journey to Jerusalem is true, we should be forced to conclude that this journey and his arrest occurred somewhere between A.D. 52-53 and 58. And as for myself, I should be willing to leave the matter thus indeterminate. But if it should be true that we had to make a more precise decision, however tentative we knew it to be, I should stand by my proposal, made in the preceding chapter, that Paul's arrest took place at about the time of the Felix-Festus succession, that this succession occurred in A.D. 55,[10] and that therefore his conversion happened twenty to twenty-one years earlier, that is, around A.D. 34. This date for the conversion, it may be said incidentally, is precisely the same as that settled on by Jewett and is only one year later than that offered as one of two alternatives by Luedemann. It now becomes possible to suggest approximate dates for the several events mentioned in our schedule a few pages back (62-63).

a. Conversion and Call to Apostleship .... A.D. 34
b. First Jerusalem Visit 37
c. Arrival in Macedonia 40
d. Arrival in Corinth 43
e. Arrival in Ephesus 46
f. Second Jerusalem Visit (Conference) 51
g. Last Visit to Corinth (Completion of Collection) 54
h. Last Visit to Jerusalem .... 54 or 55

We cannot leave this discussion of the chronology of Paul's life without dealing somewhat with two chronological statements furnished us by Acts to which we have so far had no occasion to refer. Both fall within the story of Paul's first visit to Corinth in Acts 18:1-18. The first of these is Luke's statement that some Jews of Corinth haled Paul before the Roman proconsul Gallio. Now an inscription found at Delphi puts beyond doubt

---

[10]See above, 46-47.

the fact that Gallio was proconsul of Achaia in A.D. 52.[11] Since he may have been in office as long as two years, and since we cannot tell whether the inscription marks a time near the beginning or ending of his term, we may estimate its possible outside limits as A.D. 50 and 54. Now obviously this datum is incompatible with the chronological scheme developed here, since according to our scheme Paul must have first reached Corinth hardly later than A.D. 45, perhaps several years earlier.

We may resolve this difficulty in either of two ways. First, there is the possibility that Luke is entirely mistaken in having Paul appear before Gallio. Such a mistake would not by any means be solitary in Luke-Acts: Luke dates Jesus' birth in the time of Herod by the census under Quirinius of Syria, although the census is virtually certain to have occurred a decade after Herod's death. Gamaliel in a speech in Acts makes chronologically mistaken allusions to two earlier Jewish revolutionaries, Judas and Theudas. If the explanation proposed on pages 36-40 of the so-called relief visit is correct, the reference to Claudius in Acts 11:28 belongs exactly in the same category with the reference to Quirinius in Luke 2:2. It is undoubtedly true that Luke takes a particular interest in correlating incidents in the story of Jesus or the church with secular political events. If he knew that Paul appeared before the governor of Achaia and knew also from some other source that Gallio was the governor at the supposed time of the appearance, he had all that he needed to produce the story in Acts 18:12-17.

The other way of resolving the difficulty is to say that Luke is correct in saying that Paul was brought before Gallio but mistaken in regarding the incident as occurring during Paul's *first* period of residence in Corinth. As a matter of fact, according to our scheme Paul was in Corinth in A.D. 53 (Rom. 15–Acts 20:3), and Luke tells us that he left the city earlier than he had intended because of a "plot by the Jews." Perhaps it was toward the end of this latest visit that he was brought before the Roman official.

The second chronological statement in this same Acts story of Paul's first visit to Corinth is the remark that when Paul arrived there, "he found a Jew named Aquila, a native of Pontus, lately come from Italy with his wife Priscilla, because Claudius had commanded all the Jews to leave Rome." Now it is an interesting fact that although the reference to Gallio creates, as we have seen, a difficulty for what may be called the letters

---

[11]The text of this inscription can be found in Adolf Deissmann, *Paul* (London: Hodder and Stoughton, 1926) appendix I.

chronology, this allusion to the edict of Claudius makes some trouble for the conventional scheme. Comparison of Suetonius (*Claudius* XXV) and Dio Cassius (LX. 6.6) indicates that the most probable date for the edict is A.D. 41, soon after the beginning of Claudius's reign.[12] "It must be admitted," writes Kirsopp Lake, "that if there were no reason to the contrary it would probably be put down to A.D. 41. Acts, however, distinctly says that Aquila and Priscilla had 'recently' arrived from Italy, and 41 is far too early to be a conceivable date for Paul in Corinth."[13] The foregoing discussion should have gone some distance toward showing that this last statement is in error. Not only is it conceivable that Paul was in Corinth not long after A.D. 41; according to the chronological plan developed in these pages it is highly probable.

Of course this reference to Claudius may well have no better foundation than the reference to the same ruler in Acts 11:28, or perhaps the reference to Gallio in 18:12. It must also be acknowledged that the evidence for A.D. 41 as the date of the expulsion of the Jews is not as strong and conclusive as is the evidence for A.D. 52 as the date for Gallio. But even so, it is worth noting that whatever support the Gallio reference may be thought of as giving the Acts chronology is at least partly offset by the support the Aquila and Priscilla reference gives the letters chronology. These two data from Luke-Acts in some degree cancel each other out.

Let it be said, before I leave the matter of the chronology of Paul's life, that I am under no illusion as to the comprehensiveness of my proposal or of its truth in detail. There are in the various letters hints of events that neither the letters nor Acts permits us to fit into any coherent scheme we can devise. Paul's words in 2 Corinthians 11:23-28 vividly remind us of how very much we do not know.

. . . with far greater labors [than other apostles], far more imprisonments, with

---

[12]It is true, as Sherman Johnson points out (*Anglican Theological Review* 23 [1941]: 175), that Dio Cassius describes Claudius's edict as forbidding the assembling of Jews but not exiling them. Johnson believes this refers to a distinct and earlier decree, but usually such divergences represent errors of historians in reporting one event, rather than two original events. It has been suggested that perhaps Claudius first excluded the Jews and then softened the edict, or that the harsher part of the edict was found unenforceable and went by default.

[13]F. J. Foakes-Jackson and Kirsopp Lake, *The Beginnings of Christianity*, pt. 1 (London: Macmillan & Co., 1933) 5:459.

countless beatings, and often near death. Five times I have received at the hands of the Jews the forty lashes less one. Three times I have been beaten with rods; once I was stoned. Three times I have been shipwrecked; a night and a day I have been adrift at sea; on frequent journeys, in danger from rivers, danger from robbers, danger from my own people, danger from Gentiles, danger in the city, danger in the wilderness, danger at sea, danger from false brethren; in toil and hardship, through many a sleepless night, in hunger and thirst, often without food, in cold and exposure. And, apart from other things, there is the daily pressure upon me of my anxiety for all the churches.

V

On the question of the chronological order of the letters of Paul our scheme has little bearing. The only requirement of the scheme itself is that Galatians should have been written *after* the conference and therefore not earlier than, say, A.D. 51. But that is where most scholars have always placed it—that is, in the period of Paul's residence in Ephesus toward the end of his active career.

Of the other letters, we can, on the basis of internal evidence alone, place five of them—1 and 2 Thessalonians, 1 and 2 Corinthians, and Romans, in that order. 1 Thess. 2:1-2, 17-18 and 3:1-2, 6-7 clearly indicate that this letter was written soon after Paul's first visit to Thessalonica, and we have seen reasons to believe that this was early in Paul's apostolic career (see p. 57). 2 Thessalonians, if genuine, can be explained as a sequel to 1 Thessalonians, although there is nothing decisive against a much later and quite indeterminate date. The Corinthian letters place themselves in the period between the second and the final visits to Jerusalem by their references to the offering then in progress (1 Cor. 16:1-4; 2 Cor. 8-9). And Romans likewise dates itself just as clearly as having been written soon after 2 Corinthians by its allusions to that same offering (15:25-33). This means that 1 and 2 Corinthians were probably written in A.D. 51-53 and Romans in A.D. 53-54. 1 Thessalonians, and presumably 2 Thessalonians, also must have been composed considerably earlier, perhaps not long after A.D. 40.

As to place of writing, 1 Corinthians was obviously composed in Asia, probably Ephesus (16:19); 2 Corinthians (that is, 1-9[14]) in Macedonia,

---

[14]2 Cor. 10-13 constitutes a problem whose solution is doubtful, except that it seems clear that these chapters were not originally a part of what we know as 2 Corinthians. It is possible also that chapters 8 and 9 were originally separate notes,

probably Philippi (2:12-14); and Romans probably in Corinth, since 2 Corinthians clearly indicates that Paul is on his way there to receive the church's offering, and Rom. 15:25-33 tells us that he has just received it. As for the Thessalonian letters, if we had only the letters we should undoubtedly place the writing of 1 Thessalonians in Athens (see 3:1-6). But there is no evidence in the letter against Corinth, where, because of Acts 18:5, these letters are usually assigned.[15]

With regard to the so-called imprisonment letters, the proposed scheme leaves us in the same uncertainty as before about both place and date. Since Colossians and Philemon reflect Paul's activities in Asia, and since Philippians (for example, 4:10, 14-16) unmistakably presupposes a long-standing relationship of Paul with that church, these letters could hardly have been earlier than the time of Paul's residence in Ephesus, say, A.D. 47-53; and since the offering is not mentioned in them, the earlier part of this period is indicated. But there is nothing decisive against the usual date, during the Roman imprisonment described at the very end of Acts. It is quite illegitimate, however, to suppose that these letters *must* have been written either in Rome or Caesarea because Acts tells of no extended imprisonment earlier and elsewhere. Paul's own reference to "far more imprisonments" in 2 Corinthians 11:23 is enough to place us on guard against reliance upon Acts on such a point, especially as emphasis upon earlier imprisonments would obviously not have served the interest of this writer in representing Christianity as being politically unobjectionable. Deissmann, Duncan[16] and others propose an imprisonment in Ephesus, and this hypothesis accords well with our suggestion of A.D. 47-50 as a possible pe-

---

or that one of them was. But it is most probable that all of this correspondence, in however many parts and whatever order, took place between A.D. 51 and 53 or 54. We know, however, from 1 Cor. 5:9 that Paul had earlier correspondence with Corinth, and it is of course not impossible that some fragments of earlier letters or of some earlier letter are preserved (as, for example, 2 Cor. 6:14-7:1).

[15]It should be noted, however, that Paul's references to Timothy's movements in 1 Thess. 3:1-6 cannot be harmonized with the statements of Acts concerning them. According to Paul he sent Timothy from Athens back to Thessalonica; according to Acts he *left* Timothy in Berea. Since Luke-Acts is mistaken in this detail, the writer may also be mistaken in saying that Paul had left Athens and had reached Corinth before Timothy returned from Macedonia.

[16]*St. Paul's Ephesian Ministry* (New York: Scribner's, 1930). George S. Duncan gives a full account of earlier literature on this possibility.

riod for these letters. But this is only one of several fairly plausible hypotheses.

Indeed, no neat scheme of the order of the letters of Paul is free from objection. For example, nothing would seem clearer than that 1 Thessalonians was written quite early in Paul's ministry in Europe and very soon after he left Thessalonica at the time of his first visit. Yet 1 Thess. 1:8-9, taken by itself, would indicate a considerably later date. (And 2:16*b*, if taken most naturally, would suggest a date outside Paul's lifetime entirely!) Likewise, 2 Cor. 12:18, in which the activities at Corinth of Titus and "the brother" are mentioned in retrospect, would seem clearly to belong to a period later than 2 Cor. 8:18-24, in which Paul is apparently introducing "the brother" to the Corinthians for the first time; and yet it is difficult to accommodate the bitter, boasting letter of 2 Cor. 10-13 in the brief period of freedom that follows 2 Cor. 8 if this chapter itself belongs with the earlier part of what we know as 2 Corinthians. Also we may wonder how Paul in Romans can be so complacent about his work "from Jerusalem and as far round as Illyricum" and can feel that he no longer has "any room for work in these regions" (Rom. 15:19, 23) so soon after the grave disturbances in Galatia and Corinth that are reflected in Galatians (if the epistle is to be placed in this period) and in 2 Cor. 10-13.

These are additional reminders both of how many gaps there are in our knowledge of the life of Paul and of how extensive the work of the editor, or of various early editors, of Paul's letters may have been.[17]

---

[17]The two most significant recent contributions to the discussion of the Pauline chronology are *A Chronology of Paul's Life* (1979) by Robert Jewett and the first volume of *Paul, Apostle to the Gentiles* (1984; the German edition was published in 1980) by Gerd Luedemann. Both books have been referred to earlier in this chapter. Luedemann faithfully follows the method of using our sources for Paul that I have been defending in this book. His work is of the greatest scholarly value, exhaustively detailed and fully documented. Needless to say, I am enormously grateful for it and differ from its author only on minor points. For Jewett's book I cannot say as much, although I have found it stimulating. He follows the traditional method for the greater part, but departs from it in recognizing the truth of the "three-visit" frame. For what they may be worth my criticisms of both books appear in *Colloquy on New Testament Studies*, ed. Bruce Corley, (Macon GA: Mercer University Press, 1983) 341-64

Chapter VI

The Man and His Work

Up to this point we have been concerned almost entirely with the formal facts of Paul's life—the kind of thing that might be included in a *Who's Who* sketch. From now on our attention will be more directly upon the man himself. In this chapter we shall be asking: What sort of man was Paul, and how did he carry on his work as an apostle? In the several chapters that follow we shall be concerned with the more intimate facts of his religious life.

Enough has already been said, perhaps, about sources for the study of the inward side of the apostle's life (see pp. 18-19). Here there will be no dispute: the letters represent virtually our only source. And this is t true, not only because the Luke-Acts account of Paul says so little of an illuminating kind about this side of his life, but also because, as we have seen, the letters say so much. Paul's letters are genuine personal letters—not the kind of literary epistle that later was to come into vogue among Christians as it was always in vogue among pagans of this general period (witness the letters of Cicero and Pliny). Moreover, Paul's letters are unusually revealing, even for letters, and convey his personality in an extraordinarily vivid and direct way. Although we may sometimes find ourselves wishing that Paul had produced a formal treatise, systematically planned and carefully composed, setting forth his thought as an organic whole, we are certain on reflection to realize that we should be incalculably poorer if such a treatise were acquired at the cost of even one of the more important of his letters. For Paul's thought is, in a peculiar sense and degree, *personal* thought—

that is, thought bound up inseparably with the man himself and deeply and pervasively affected by the quality of his experiences. It is therefore, we may believe, not an accident, as it is certainly not a misfortune, that what we know of Paul's thought comes to us in letters. Even for the study of his theology such sources are good; for the study of the man himself we could not hope for better. We could wish only that there were more of them.

I

The only description we have of the personal appearance of Paul is found in the Acts of Paul, a book dating from the end of the second century. The writer of that book describes the apostle as "a man little of stature, partly bald, with crooked legs, of vigorous physique, with eyes set close together and nose somewhat hooked." Since this book is as a whole fanciful in the extreme, it is highly unlikely that this picture is anything more than the author's mental image. To be sure, the description is in some degree supported by a remark that Paul quotes from some of his opponents: "His letters are weighty and strong, but his bodily presence is weak, and his speech of no account" (2 Cor. 10:10). Allowing for some doubt as to the exact meaning of the middle clause of this sentence as well as for the fact that the whole sentence is quoted from his opponents, we are bound to conclude that Paul was less than distinguished in his physical presence. However, when one calls him "an ugly little Jew," as has been done, one goes beyond what any intimation of a good source justifies.

The same thing can be said of the frequent assertion that Paul was a sickly, if not a chronically ill, man. Such an assertion rests only upon a casual remark of Paul that an illness of his provided the occasion of his first contact with those who became his converts in Galatia (Gal. 4:13) and upon some rather enigmatic words of his in 2 Cor. 12:7-9a: "To keep me from being too elated by the abundance of revelations, a thorn was given me in the flesh, a messenger of Satan, to harass me, to keep me from being too elated. Three times I besought the Lord about this, that it should leave me; but he said to me, 'My grace is sufficient for you, for my power is made perfect in weakness.' " It has been generally surmised that this thorn in the flesh could only mean a physical ailment, and the guesses as to what it was have included malaria, excessive nervousness, epilepsy and near blindness. Joseph Klausner makes a vigorous argument for epilepsy on the basis not only of the passages just cited but also of the many indications that Paul was of an ecstatic temperament and susceptible of vivid mystical experiences. Klausner quotes from modern writers to show the ecstatic character of the epileptic's trances. Dostoyevski, an epileptic, is quoted as saying in describing an attack, "I felt as if heaven came down to earth and swallowed me up. I literally received God into myself and was filled with Him." "Here," adds Klausner, "in these remarkable words is to be sought the key to the vision of Paul."[1] But how Paul could call the occasion, if not the source, of such experiences a "thorn . . . in the flesh, a messenger of Satan," Klausner does not say. As a matter of fact, we do not have the remotest idea what Paul's ailment was, how long he suffered it, whether the suffering was chronic or intermittent, or whether indeed it was an ailment at all. Whatever it was, however, we certainly are not justified in thinking of Paul as sickly. In the catalogue of his sufferings in 2 Cor. 11:23-29 he does not mention illness. Surely that long list of labors, exposures, deprivations and dangers hardly suggests an invalid! At several other points in his letters we should have expected a reference to his illness if he had been greatly troubled by it. The evidence on the whole supports at this point the statement of the author of the Acts of Paul: "of vigorous physique."

It is interesting to note the evidence in 2 Cor. 10:10 that Paul was not a good speaker: "His letters are weighty and strong," his enemies say, "but his bodily presence is weak, and his speech of no account." The reference of this last clause is almost certainly to Paul's manner of speaking rather than to the substance of his speech. Thus Goodspeed renders it, "As a speaker he amounts to nothing"; and Moffatt, "His delivery is beneath contempt." Several paragraphs farther on Paul again refers to this criticism of him, perhaps intending to acknowledge that it has some truth, when he says, "Even if I am unskilled in speaking, I am not in knowledge" (2 Cor. 11:6). And it is strongly indicated in Paul's first letter to Corinth that he was sometimes unfavorably compared with more eloquent men among the apostles (for example, 1 Cor. 2:1-5) and that such comparisons gave him some pain, perhaps the more because he was aware of his shortcomings in this regard.

What makes this little item most interesting is the fact that the book of Acts gives so radically different a picture. No one would have been likely to say about the orator of Mars Hill or before Agrippa, "As a speaker he amounts to nothing." Those addresses ascribed to Paul are skillful and el-

---

[1]Joseph Klausner, *From Jesus to Paul* (New York: Macmillan, 1943) 328-29.

oquent, and we get the impression that they were delivered in the same way, skillfully and eloquently. We can almost hear Paul's calm but ringing tones and see his stately gestures when, having "stretched out his hand," he "made his defense" before Agrippa. It is inconceivable that Luke thought of Paul as speaking otherwise than ably, impressively and in the most approved fashion. We have, then, this rather fascinating situation: Paul's letters represent him as a forceful and effective writer but as having few gifts as a speaker; Acts, on the other hand, presents him as an able orator but makes nothing of his letters—indeed does not give the slightest hint that he wrote any at all (see p. 11, esp. n. 6). There is, of course, no question of which source we should follow at this point—and at every other where there is any disparity—but it is interesting to speculate on the significance of this curious reversal.

It should perhaps go without saying that whatever Paul lacked in oratorical skill was more than compensated for by the earnestness and vividness of his speech, not to mention the sheer force of his gospel. We are likely to picture him speaking with many nervous gestures, in emotionally charged tones, with eyes burning, with face mobile and aglow—himself completely dominated by what he is saying and become a completely surrendered medium for the communication of it to others. Such a speaker can be ungraceful, even uncouth, according to all the rules of speech and still be powerfully persuasive. That Paul was such a speaker can be gathered, not only from the way he expresses himself in his letters, but also from the fact that despite his lack of oratorical skill he actually proved to be mightily effective. The results of his preaching put that fact beyond question. "When I came to you, brethren," he writes to his converts at Corinth, "[it was] in weakness and in much fear and trembling; and my speech and my message were not in plausible words of wisdom, but in demonstration of the Spirit and power, that your faith might not rest in the wisdom of men but in the power of God." This may be in part an attempt on Paul's part to justify himself for failing with some of his hearers—to rationalize a lack of learning and eloquence of which he was somewhat ashamed. But it is also undoubtedly a sober account of the effectiveness of his preaching, at Corinth and elsewhere. It was indeed in "Spirit and power." However undistinguished or even unprepossessing he may have been in his appearance, and however lacking in the gifts and skills of the orator, he did not force a passage for the gospel from Syria to the shores of the Adriatic by his letters alone, for all their weight and strength!

II

We know that Paul was greatly loved and greatly hated. Both facts are to be gathered from his letters and are strongly seconded by the Acts story. That book, to be sure, in line with its "catholic" tendency, finds Paul's enemies entirely among "the Jews," but the letters make clear that some of these Jews were also Christians and that their opposition to him was quite as bitter as that of their unbelieving brethren.[2] Just as throughout most of the second century Paul was a major center of controversy in the church—as indeed he has been in a less conspicuous way ever since—so it was in his own lifetime. In fact, as we have already noted (p. 35), the bitter quarrel between Marcionite and catholic at the middle of the second century is by no means unrelated to the bitter quarrel between Paul and certain Jewish Christians at the middle of the first. Paul's life was lived in the midst of conflict. He speaks of "fighting without and fear within" (2 Cor. 7:5), and that phrase (to which we shall briefly return) goes far to explain some of the curious paradoxes of character that the letters reveal. That Paul had many antagonists and, it is also clear, many protagonists is attributable to certain controversial convictions that can more appropriately be discussed in another connection, but that he was also loved and hated tells us something about the temperament and character of the man himself.

There can be no doubt that he was loved by many. It is true that we do not have any direct evidence of this. No written expressions of loyalty or affection toward him have come down to us. How fortunate it would have been, in many more ways than this, if in the fashion of other collectors and publishers of epistles the original collector of Paul's letters had included some of the letters the apostle received as well as those he dispatched—for example, the communication from Corinth to which Paul refers in 1 Cor. 7:1. Even without such evidence, however, one can be quite sure not only of the esteem in which he was held by many in his churches, but also of their affection as well. This warm regard is reflected unmistakably in such parts of his correspondence as 1 Thessalonians, 2 Corinthians (1-9) and Philippians—indeed, to some extent in all of his letters. And Paul's references to his associates, to such men as Titus and Timothy, are often such as to indicate their love for him almost as clearly as his for them. In

---

[2]In 2 Cor. 11:26, along with "dangers" from Gentiles, from Jews, from the wilderness and the sea, Paul can speak of "dangers from false brethren."

other words, Paul also (like his own Master) had his disciples, who besides acknowledging his authority as a teacher and accepting his interpretation of the gospel were warmly and deeply attached to his person. It was one of these who almost certainly took the initiative in collecting his letters a generation after his death. This loyalty on their part toward him answered, of course, to his own affection for his converts and "fellow-workers," which is more directly expressed in the letters.

It is important to emphasize this character of Paul's relationships because it is so often slighted or ignored. Many moderns have so *disliked* Paul that they do not realize that many of his contemporaries *loved* him. He is not infrequently pictured as a fanatic incapable of feeling or eliciting affection. The letters not only do not justify such a picture; they give just the opposite impression. One who reads them with this particular issue in mind will be amazed at the number and extent of the passages concerned entirely with expressing Paul's own feelings towards his churches—whether of tender solicitude when they were being tried, of grief over their failures or sufferings, or of joy over their triumphs. In his exhortation, "Love one another with brotherly affection. . . . Rejoice with those who rejoice, weep with those who weep" (Rom. 12:10, 15), there is every reason to believe Paul was but preaching what he also practiced. And no one would have been able to write 1 Cor. 13 who had not himself walked in that "more excellent way."

It cannot be denied that there is an element of jealous pride in Paul's affection. His love is not altogether disinterested; it is not pure *agape*. He wants his converts to stand firm, not only in the Lord, but also in their loyalty to him. He is genuinely distressed by the divisions at Corinth and nobly associates himself with Cephas and Apollos as mere "servants through whom you believed. . . . I planted, Apollos watered, . . . but [it is] only God who gives the growth. He who plants and he who waters are equal" (1 Cor. 3:5-8; see also 1:12). But it soon appears that, although Paul deprecates the parties, he is inclined on the whole to favor the party of Paul. He is absolutely sincere in his desire that his converts shall not place loyalty to Paul above loyalty to Christ, but he is obviously not ready to tolerate easily their feeling a superior loyalty to any other human leader. "For though you have countless guides in Christ, you do not have many fathers. For I became your father in Christ Jesus through the gospel" (1 Cor. 4:15). This intense desire for the loyalty and love of his own churches lies back of his boast of not building on another's foundation. He carefully refrains from working in another's field partly in order to be in position to claim autonomy in his own. We must suppose, therefore, that when in this same passage in 1 Corinthians (3:10) he says, "According to the commission of God given to me, like a skilled master-builder I laid a foundation, and another man is building upon it," he is expressing some measure of disapproval of this other "man." Paul himself, the implication is, did not thus intrude into another's "field" or "building." Paul probably did not recognize that one reason he did not do so was his selfish pleasure and pride in possessing entirely, or at least largely, the devotion of his own churches.

But only more of a saint than we have the right to expect anyone to be could under the circumstances have kept his love of his churches free from any such taint of selfishness and pride. Besides, his jealousy for them was often in no small part a jealousy for the truth and for Christ, since loyalty to another leader would sometimes have meant loyalty to quite a different "gospel" (Gal. 1:6), which as Paul saw it, was not a gospel at all. In any case, and with whatever mixture of motives, Paul identified himself completely not only with the gospel he preached but also with the people who were led to accept it under his ministry. He could refer to his message as "my gospel," and he thought of the people also as being in a very peculiar sense his own. If he took a selfish pride in them, he was also willing to accept any sacrifice their welfare demanded of him. "Who is weak, and I am not weak? Who is made to fall, and I am not indignant?" (2 Cor. 11:29).

III

Paul's indignation could wax warm indeed. At times it seems to get entirely out of hand, and he expresses himself in harsh, even brutal, terms, which he must later have regretted. But it is only when we see his anger in the context provided by his self-identification with his churches that we are in position truly to interpret it. Contrary to frequently expressed opinion, Paul was not by temperament irascible or pugnacious. There are many evidences of this, besides the generally affectionate and generous tone of his letters. He tells us that he has endeavored to be "all things to all men" that he "might by all means save some" (1 Cor. 9:22). Anyone who sees in this statement a sign that Paul was a thoroughgoing opportunist, willing to make any conceivable concession in the interest of harmony, is as mistaken as he who makes Paul out to be the congenital antagonist, "sudden and quick in quarrel," implacable and unyielding. Nevertheless, he was, as to most things, eager to be conciliatory and rather expert in being so.

The "thanksgivings" of Paul's letters (the sections that regularly follow the salutations) are models of courtesy, and scattered through his correspondence are many passages of exquisite charm. Sometimes it may seem to the modern reader that Paul must often have offended by presuming too much upon the esteem, affection and reverence of his readers, as he chides, exhorts or praises them very much in the manner of a parent with little children. But we do not know enough about his churches and about his relations with them to justify any such supposition. A strong presumption that he did not write without due regard to the psychological realities—that is, did not ignore or misjudge what would seem appropriate and be acceptable to his readers—is created by the fact that in writing the church at Rome, which he did not establish and with which he was not acquainted, he carefully avoids a parental, or even a pastoral, tone. The little letter to Philemon is full of quite charming compliments, and the phrase "beloved both as a man and in the Lord" shows us that Paul was able to appreciate natural as well as Christian graces. It is likely that if we had a larger number of Paul's more personal letters—that is, letters not concerned primarily with the problems of churches—we should be in less danger of missing the warmth of his friendliness and the charm and tact that were major traits of his character.

The impression that Paul was most characteristically the fighter is based almost entirely upon two of his letters, Galatians and 2 Cor. 10-13. But these letters were not improbably written in the same brief period—when the controversy with the Judaizers was in an acute phase—and reveal Paul in a mood both unusual and essentially uncongenial. So far as the letters give us any indication, it would seem that Paul's indignation was stirred deeply by only two things: one of these was any effort to bring his converts into what he called bondage to the Jewish law[3] and the other was any effort to undermine his own position in the regard of his churches. When these two occasions coincided, as in the Judaizers' propaganda, Paul's anger knew no limits.

From what we can gather concerning the methods of Paul's enemies, it would appear that he had ample temptation to anger. Apparently, besides insisting that Paul did not have the authority of an apostle and that

---

[3]Paul may be assumed to have had the same kind of anger against the Christians before his conversion and for the same reason: in each case he sees a group engaged in destroying God's people.

insofar as his message differed from that of certain preferred teachers (presumably some of Jesus' original disciples) it had no value, they made quite vicious personal attacks. We have already noted their aspersions upon his appearance and upon his gifts as a speaker. They accused him of being boastful and overbearing, of robbing some churches in order to be in position to pretend in others that he worked for nothing, and of being dishonest in his administration of church funds. Paul resists these attacks with no holds barred. He calls his opponents "false apostles, deceitful workmen," comparing them with Satan himself (2 Cor. 11:13-14). He alludes to them as "the dogs" (Phil. 3:2), refers to the rite of circumcision as a mutilation, and on one occasion goes so far as to express the wish that those who are insisting that the Gentile believers must accept circumcision would in their own persons go further and "have themselves emasculated" (Gal. 5:12, Goodspeed). Such language is about as harsh as could be imagined and comes strangely from a "saint"!

Only a blind reader of Paul's epistles could miss the signs of the egoism and pride that are behind this indignation. At the same time, we shall do well to realize that in this particular controversy there was more than the ordinary temptation to identify the cause of truth with one's own cause and to resist attacks on oneself as being attacks on Christ. Paul's opponents had been first to identify Paul himself—his own character and calling—with his cause. He was therefore often, although certainly not always, justified in regarding an attack on his authority as involving also an attack upon what he conceived to be the heart of the gospel, namely, the availability of the salvation in Christ to everyone who had faith, whether Jew or Greek. There can be no doubt of the crucial importance of the issue or of the debt we owe to Paul as the great protagonist of a Christianity free from racial or national restrictions. He was—not merely in his own egoistic fancy, but in fact—the personal symbol of the position he defended. Who under such circumstances would have been able always to discriminate between what he wanted for Christ's sake and what he wanted for his own?

But fighting was not a congenial activity of Paul's. He did not like a fight, as some men seem to. There is a sentence in one of Pliny's letters in which, after appealing to a slave's master to forgive and receive back an offending slave, he says, "Concede something to his youth, to his tears, and to your own natural mildness of temper; do not make him uneasy any longer, and I will add, too, do not make yourself so, for a man of your kindness of heart cannot be angry without feeling great uneasiness."[4] Does not Paul come near to the meaning of this last clause when he speaks of "fighting without and fear within"? His sometimes hysterical words in controversy and his often ugly boasting are perhaps signs of this inner "uneasiness." He was in his true and natural character a man of peace.

IV

Paul was obviously of a strongly emotional temperament. He was subject to moods of great elation and of deep despondency. Not infrequently this characteristic of the apostle is associated with his mysticism, for mystics are typically susceptible to such extremes of feeling. It is obvious that Paul was something of a mystic, but he was not a mystic in the ordinary sense, nor are his moods the characteristic moods of the mystic. The latter are inwardly determined: sometimes God is real and present; sometimes he is unreal and remote. A period of great inner joy is likely to be succeeded by a period of dryness and depression. This alternation of feelings takes place with no reference, or with the sightest possible reference, to anything happening in the social environment of the mystic. There are no signs in Paul's letters that he was subject to moods of this kind.

On one occasion, it is true, Paul mentions his elation in connection with "visions and revelations of the Lord" (2 Cor. 12:1), and there can be no question that he was frequently uplifted by such experiences. He also refers to his own speaking "in ecstasy" (1 Cor. 14:18), Goodspeed). But such phenomena, while denoting a certain emotional character, do not need to mean the typical experiences of the mystic. Insofar as Paul was subject to changing moods of despondency and joy, they seem to have been dependent not upon the presence or absence of these "revelations"—although he set great store by them and found great significance in them—but upon more overt occasions.

This can be readily illustrated. Paul tells us that after leaving Thessalonica at the end of his first visit he was so unhappy that he could not rest. But the reason for this unhappiness was anxiety about what might have happened to the church there. He tells us that when he could "bear it no longer," he sent Timothy to find out. Now as he writes 1 Thessalonians, he is in one of the most joyous moods reflected in his correspondence: "Now that Timothy has come to us from you, and has brought us the good

---

[4]*Letters*, trans. F. C. T. Bosanquet (London, 1914) 9:21.

news of your faith and love . . . , now we live.'' His elation is the elation of relief from a rather terrible anxiety, but both anxiety and relief have their occasion in outward circumstances. Exactly the same thing is revealed by 2 Corinthians. Paul has been temporarily estranged from his church at Corinth, or is in danger of being so; he has sent Titus with a strong letter, written, Paul says, "out of much affliction and anguish of heart and with many tears"; he now waits in Ephesus with quite pathetic eagerness for Titus's return. Unable to bear his impatience longer, he starts to meet him. He writes,

> When I came to Troas to preach the gospel of Christ, a door was opened for me in the Lord; but my mind could not rest because I did not find my brother Titus there. So I took leave of them and went on to Macedonia.
>
> . . .
>
> Even when we came into Macedonia, our bodies had no rest but we were afflicted at every turn—fighting without and fear within. But God, who comforts the downcast, comforted us by the coming of Titus, and not only by his coming but also by the comfort with which he was comforted in you, as he told us of your longing, your mourning, your zeal for me, so that I rejoiced still more (2 Cor. 2:12-13; 7:5-7).

It would appear that Paul's unhappiness is usually the unhappiness of anxiety and fear induced by some threat to the welfare of his churches or to the security of his relationship with one or more of them. We are not told what caused "the affliction [he] experienced in Asia" in which he was "so utterly, unbearably crushed that [he] despaired of life itself" (2 Cor. 1:8), but we can be sure it had some overt occasion, as indeed the context rather clearly indicates. Correspondingly, his moods of happiness seem dependent upon the security and growth of his churches and upon their love for him. They were his "joy and crown" (Phil. 4:1). He can even say, "What is our hope or joy or crown of boasting before our Lord Jesus at his coming? Is it not you? For you are our glory and joy" (1 Thess. 2:19-20). Paul claims to have "learned, in whatever state [he is], to be content." That may well be true as regards the relative abundance or lack of merely physical comforts, the matter under consideration in this passage (Phil. 4:11-12), but it is decidedly not true altogether. Paul has none of the apathy of the Stoic or the kind of transcendence we associate with the mystic or the hero. His feelings, in fact, are more than ordinarily dependent upon the propitiousness of his environment: "Who is weak, and I am not weak? Who is made to fall, and I am not indignant?" (2 Cor. 11:29).

V

For a man with something of the temperament of the ecstatic, Paul shows an amazing capacity for sound and sober judgment in practical affairs. This side of the apostle's many-sided personality appears as we listen to his answers to the questions that the church at Corinth asked him (1 Cor. 7:1ff.) or watch him deal with other difficulties there, at Thessalonica or elsewhere. Paul was more than an evangelist. We have seen that when he reached Ephesus, some nine years, perhaps, after his first visit to Jerusalem and the beginning of his work in Asia Minor, he probably made it his permanent headquarters for further work. During the preceding years he had staked out a field—churches had been established in Galatia (perhaps elsewhere in Asia Minor to the east or north of Asia), in Macedonia and in Greece. Ephesus lay near the center of this field, and from that center Paul could effectively superintend his churches. He had become, in all but name, the bishop of a large diocese. Undoubtedly, he continued to do evangelistic preaching, but the spreading of the gospel into new areas within his field could obviously be done more effectively by the local churches. Thus it would be from Philippi and Thessalonica that the movement spread into other parts of Macedonia, and Corinth would be the base of operations for the evangelization of Achaia. Paul found himself increasingly occupied with the problems of the pastor and the administrator.

Reference has already been made to his assistants. We do not know how many of these there were, how continuously they served Paul, or in detail what their duties were. From casual references we gather the names Timothy, Titus, Silvanus, Epaphras, Aristarchus, Mark, Jesus Justus and Epaphroditus. All of these are definitely described or identified as "fellow-workers"; so also is Philemon. It is probable that Luke and Demas were also associates in work, although that is nowhere expressly said. Almost certainly Onesimus was destined to become an assistant. There were no doubt others whose names do not happen to have been mentioned. It is not to be supposed that all of these men were with Paul all the time. Indeed, Philemon is manifestly at Colossae, or Laodicea, when the letter to him is written. Titus is mentioned as present only in 2 Corinthians, and Silvanus only in 1 and 2 Thessalonians. There is more continuous evidence of Timothy's association with Paul. As to the duties of these associates, it is clear that they visited areas of Paul's field, brought reports or communications to him from his churches, served as messengers for his own letters, no doubt assisted him in the writing of them, and during periods of his imprisonments or of special stress served him in more personal ways. Perhaps they were able to assist Paul in his work as a tentmaker, on which he largely depended for his own support and, perhaps also, for the support of his associates, although it is on the whole more likely that they had their own sources of income.

All in all, one gets the impression that Paul was involved toward the end of his career in administrative operations of no small scope and complexity, and there is no indication in the letters that he did not conduct this phase of his work smoothly and efficiently.

We have more evidence concerning his way of handling the various problems with which his churches were constantly confronting him. Here our principal source is 1 Corinthians, but there is no reason to suppose that the difficulties at Corinth were peculiar to that church. Among the issues Paul might be called on to handle were Jew-Gentile relations, threats of schism, disorders in services of worship, irregularities in the observance of the Lord's Supper, a misunderstanding between two members of a local church, unhealthy excitement about the end of the world, litigation between Christians, occasional instances of serious immorality, the question of whether a Christian could eat food that had been consecrated by pagan rites, innumerable problems connected with marriage, the role of women in the church, various false teachings, the administration of charity by the churches, relations of Christians with their pagan neighbors and how Christian slaves and masters should treat each other. A generation later, rules governing most such matters had been developed by the growing church, and later still, comprehensive manuals had been produced; but Paul must perforce deal independently and for the first time with these questions. It will be agreed by most readers that he did so with patience, with common sense, and with wisdom.

To be sure, Paul had his serious limitations as a counselor. We look in vain for any sign of humor in Paul's letters. He would have been both happier and wiser if he could sometimes have laughed at and with himself and at and with others; perhaps he did, but surely not often enough, since in that case at least an occasional chuckle would have found its way into his letters. Paul also shows a surprising lack of appreciation for the spiritual possibilities in the marriage relationship, in fact, a rather abysmal and embarrassing ignorance of the total meaning of marriage. At certain other points he shares the common limitations of his age and group; he has accepted without criticism certain conventional ideas about the behavior of women; he believes that the end of the age is imminent, and that therefore there is no point in attempting radical changes in society or in one's own station; he has certain magical notions, such as that some have died at Corinth because they received the Lord's Supper "in an unworthy manner" (1 Cor. 11:27-30); he is quite naive in his attitude toward alleged gifts of the Spirit, never doubting the divine origin of the "gift of tongues," even when certain ecstatics are selfishly monopolizing the meetings of the church and denying to others with less spectacular but more useful gifts any opportunity either for self-expression or for service.

On the other hand, Paul reveals an amazing capacity for transcending these limitations or, at any rate, for finding a way through them. He believes in the imminent end of the age as vividly as does anyone at Thessalonica, but he knows that the excited, irresponsible behavior of some of the people there is inappropriate and wrong. He fully believes in the divine endowment of the ecstatics, but he also knows that it is better, at least in church, to speak "five words with my mind" than "ten thousand words in a tongue." And he can recognize that more spiritual, that is, more Spirit-caused, than either tongues or prophecy is the love that "vaunteth not itself, is not puffed up, . . . seeketh not her own." In a word, where his doctrine clashes with the facts, he does not always renounce, or even modify, his doctrine; but on the other hand, he does not refuse to face and allow for the facts. Undoubtedly the most important example of this view is Paul's doctrine that the believer in Christ is no longer under the law but under grace. That doctrine did not prevent Paul from insisting with the greatest earnestness upon the ethical obligations of Christians. Antinomianism might be the logical implication of his doctrine, but Paul had too much respect for the moral facts to draw that inference. He would rather be inconsistent in his theory than wrong about his facts. Of course, he did not recognize such inconsistencies; if he had, his theories themselves might, in some cases, have been more adequate. But we must give him a large amount of credit for a certain honesty and realism, which are, after all, more important than a merely logical consistency.

One who attempts to apply principles to actual human situations can never be perfectly consistent, no matter how adequate and appropriate his or her principles may be. Casuistry necessarily involves compromise, of logic, if not also of virtue. For this reason we often pretend nobly to despise it. But the function of the casuist is indispensable if, on the one hand, actual persons are to be given actual guidance in actual situations and, on the other, moral principles are to be anything else than abstract, irrelevant ideas to which we give a merely intellectual or sentimental assent. Paul did not despise or evade his responsibilities as a casuist. He was ready to deal with persons just where they were. The unprejudiced reader of such a passage as 1 Cor. 7:1-14:40 will be impressed by the wisdom with which he did so.

VI

There are many indications, however, that Paul did not particularly relish this role of superintendent of churches, either in its administrative or in its teaching and counseling aspects. He told the Corinthians that he had been called, not even to baptize, only to preach the gospel. He was by endowment and calling the evangelist. At the very end of the catalogue of his sufferings (2 Cor. 11:23-29) he places "the daily pressure upon me of my anxiety for all the churches"—as though that were a more grievous burden than any number of shipwrecks or beatings. He says that he has not wanted to build on another's foundations; it seems clear that he did not really enjoy building even on his own. We undoubtedly touch here a conflict in Paul's mind: on the one hand, he found pastoral and administrative work irksome; on the other, he did not want others taking his place in the life of the churches he had begun. Thus he was unwilling to be merely the evangelist; he had to remain near his churches long enough to establish them firmly and to determine the general lines of their further growth.

But he was at heart the itinerant, the pioneer. His eyes were on the distant frontier beyond which the gospel had not yet penetrated. Nowhere does this appear more strikingly than at the time when Paul feels he can safely and properly leave, at any rate for a long period, the shores of the Aegean. He is writing to the church at Rome on the eve of his departure for Jerusalem, Rome, and Spain. He tells how long he has wanted to move on westward. He has so far "been hindered" (Rom. 15:22), but now he plans his trip, "since I no longer have any room for work in these regions." What an astounding statement! Paul is alluding to a territory that he has just described, with only a little exaggeration, as extending "from Jerusalem and as far around as Illyricum"—a territory of some 300,000 square miles. No more room for work in these regions! There speaks the evangelist. There speaks the man who said, "Woe to me if I do not preach the gospel!" One can sense his deep relief as he turns his back upon money-raising, petty peacemaking, trying to answer all sorts of, to him, rather unimportant and impertinent questions, and faces toward the open west again. To be sure, he has to make this trip to Jerusalem to place what he believes will be the seal upon his work thus far. But then he will be free to do the thing God really called him to do.

This is the last sure glimpse of Paul the letters give us. This glimpse of a Paul relieved and full of hope deepens the pathos of the story of the final years of his career as the book of Acts recounts it. But, in a way in which he could not have known, his hopes were after all to be fulfilled. His letters were destined to carry the voice of the greatest of all the preachers of the gospel to "borders of the west" far beyond his farthest dream.

Part 3

The Man in Christ

Chapter VII

□────────────────────□

The Initial Revelation

We have thus far merely taken for granted what is the most manifest, and unquestionably the most decisive, fact in Paul's life, whether "outer" or "inner": the fact of Christ. Any consideration of this fact and of its meaning for Paul has been delayed until now, partly because it so obviously deserves a place of its own in this discussion—and that place the final or climactic one—but also because one is certain to be both hesitant to venture into an area of the apostle's experience so central and intimate, and reluctant to attempt, with poor tools of insight and expression, any interpretation of what might be found there. On the other hand, we must recognize not only that the meaning of Christ for Paul provides the only, and the indispensable, clue to any knowledge we may have of the man and his thought, but also that Paul himself was constantly seeking to interpret this meaning to others—"Our mouth is open to you," he writes; "our heart is wide" (2 Cor. 6:11). He thus invites us, as any serious attempt to understand him compels us, to ask what he means when he refers to himself as "a man in Christ."

I

The answer to this question, which will occupy us in these last three chapters, may well begin with emphasis upon the significance of this open attitude on the part of the apostle. His knowledge of Christ, although the deepest and most intimate fact of his life, is not a personal secret possession. He does not regard it as something unique or solitary. It is a knowledge that he possesses as a member of the Christian community. He never speaks of himself as being ''in Christ'' in any way in which every other believer is not also ''in Christ.'' The meaning of Christ is a shared meaning—the basis of that particular *koinonia,* or community, that is the church.

The consistency and faithfulness with which Paul concerns himself with this shared meaning are the more remarkable in view of the fact that he was, as we have seen, something of an ecstatic and, therefore, subject to highly individual mystical experiences. In 2 Cor. 12:1 he refers to ''visions and revelations of the Lord'' that have been granted him, and in 1 Cor. 14:18 he mentions ecstasies that the Spirit has sometimes induced. But such private experiences, although he obviously finds a certain satisfaction, even pride, in them, Paul alludes to with surprising reticence— indeed almost with a certain shame, as though he realizes that they do not belong to the deepest and most authentic meaning of Christ and that, therefore, it is not really appropriate to mention them in that connection. He knows that such experiences have the effect of separating him from other believers (and that this is why in his pride he is tempted to mention them), whereas the meaning of Christ is essentially both a humbling and a unifying meaning—not less but more profound for each for being shared by all.

Nowhere in Paul's letters is this distinction more clearly made than in his discussion of the spiritual gifts at Corinth, which we have already noted in a somewhat similar connection. Certain persons there with the gift of tongues had gone far toward destroying the peace and order of the church. It is possible that persons with other gifts had also been aggressive and divisive, but apparently the ecstatics were the chief offenders. Paul, as we have seen, does not think of denying the divine origin of these gifts or the importance of the contribution each of them is intended to make to the life of the church. He does in effect deny, however, that any of them belong intrinsically to the life in Christ. This life consists essentially of love (*agape*), and this *agape* is by definition not a private possession, but a shared-in reality, a *koinonia,* a community of life. The several private or esoteric endowments may be ''gifts of the Spirit,'' but *agape* itself *is* the Spirit. They may contribute to the enlightenment and growth of the church, but *agape* is the very reality of the church. They may be signs of Christ's resurrection, but *agape* is the presence of Christ himself.

Thus, to answer our question in a very summary fashion, we may say that when Paul speaks of himself as ''a man in Christ, '' he refers to the fact that he has, by God's grace, been made a part of that ultimate, eschatological order, that divine community of love, which in the Gospels is called the kingdom of God and which is already proleptically and partially present among us as the church, whose "spirit" (that is, the inner principle that constitutes and distinguishes it) authenticates itself both as the Spirit of God and as the continuing reality and presence of Christ. The meaning of such a statement obviously needs to be elaborated and defined, and much of this section will be devoted to the attempt to do so. First, however, we must consider the way in which the apostle's Christian life began. What can we know of the circumstances and the inner meaning of what is ordinarily called his conversion?

II

At the outset we shall do well to have clearly in mind the biblical passages in which this experience is explicitly mentioned. There are three of these in Acts and three in the letters and all of them are brief enough to permit being quoted in full.

The Letters

For I would have you know, brethren, that the gospel which was preached by me is not man's gospel. For I did not receive it from man, nor was I taught it, but it came through a revelation of Jesus Christ. For you have heard of my former life in Judaism, how I persecuted the church of God violently and tried to destroy it; and I advanced in Judaism beyond many of my own age among my people, so extremely zealous was I for the traditions of my fathers. But when he who had set me apart before I was born, and had called me through his grace, was pleased to reveal his Son to me, in order that I might preach him among the Gentiles, I did not confer with flesh and blood. (Gal. 1:11-16)

Am I not free? Am I not an apostle? Have I not seen Jesus our Lord? Are not you my workmanship in the Lord? If to others I am not an apostle, at least I am to you. (1 Cor. 9:1-2)

For I delivered to you as of first importance what I also received, that Christ died for our sins in accordance with the scriptures, that he was buried, that he was raised on the third day in accordance with the scriptures, and that he appeared to Cephas, then to the twelve. Then he appeared to more than five hundred brethren at one time, most of whom are still alive, though some have fallen asleep. Then he appeared to James, then to all the apostles. Last of all, as to one untimely born, he appeared also to me. For I am the least of the apostles, unfit to be called an apostle, because I persecuted the church of God. But by the grace of God I am what I am, and his grace toward me was not in vain. On the contrary, I worked harder than any of them, though it was not I but the grace of God which is with me. Whether then it was I or they, so we preach and so you believe. (1 Cor. 15:3-11)

Acts

But Saul, still breathing threats and murder against the disciples of the Lord, . . . approached Damascus, and suddenly a light from heaven flashed about him. And he fell to the ground and heard a voice saying to him, "Saul, Saul, why do you persecute me?" And he said, "Who are you, Lord?" And he said, "I am Jesus, whom you are persecuting; but rise and enter the city, and you will be told what you are to do." The men who were traveling with him stood speechless, hearing the voice but seeing no one. (9:1-7)

As I made my journey and drew near to Damascus, about noon a great light from heaven suddenly shone about me. And I fell to the ground and heard a voice saying to me, "Saul, Saul, why do you persecute me?" And I answered, "Who are you, Lord?" And he said to me, "I am Jesus of Nazareth whom you are persecuting." Now those who were with me saw the light but did not hear the voice of the one who was speaking to me. And I said, "What shall I do, Lord?" And the Lord said to me, "Rise, and go into Damascus, and there you will be told all that is appointed for you to do." (22:6-10)

Thus I journeyed to Damascus. . . . At midday, O king, I saw on the way a light from heaven, brighter than the sun, shining round me and those who journeyed with me. And when we had all fallen to the ground, I heard a voice saying to me in the Hebrew language, "Saul, Saul, why do you persecute me? It hurts you to kick against the goads." And I said, "Who are you, Lord?" And the Lord said, "I am Jesus whom you are persecuting. But rise and stand upon your feet; for I have appeared to you for this purpose, to appoint you to serve and bear witness to the things in which you have seen me and to those in which I will appear to you." (26:12-16)

We note at once certain points of agreement between the several Acts descriptions of the experience on the one hand and Paul's references on the other. We have already observed the fact that Damascus (or near Damascus) figures in both sources (see above, pp. 23-24). It is also indicated by both Acts and Paul that this experience came soon after, if not in the midst of, his activity as a persecutor, and that its effects were immediate and revolutionary. In both it stands forth clearly as the radical turning point in

Paul's career—not only does the unbeliever suddenly become the believer, but the persecutor becomes the protagonist. This is the major emphasis of all three passages in Acts, of course, and the fact is placed beyond any doubt by Paul's own words in Gal. 1:11-16.

At this point, however, parallelism between the two sets of accounts ceases. The several Acts descriptions tell of Paul's falling to the ground, of his seeing a great light, and of a conversation between Paul and Jesus. We also read that Paul had companions at the time, and we are given a rather confused impression of their reaction to this incident: in one story they "stood speechless, hearing the voice but seeing no one"; in the second they "saw the light but did not hear the voice"; in the third the light shone round the whole company, and all fell to the ground. Paul, on the other hand, mentions none of the circumstances of this catastrophic, transforming experience. This silence, of course, cannot be taken as discrediting the Acts story. There is nothing in Paul's letters that casts any necessary doubt upon the presence of companions, or upon the light, or the voice. It is noteworthy, however, that the one assertion Paul *does* make about the character of the experience has no parallel in any of the Acts accounts. The one thing—and the only thing—Paul says about the experience is that he saw the Lord. Not only do the Acts accounts not mention this fact, they all but exclude it.[1]

The significance of this discrepancy can be seen only in light of the very special value Paul attached to this particular feature of his experience—if we can use the word "feature" to designate what was for Paul its whole essential character. Both Luke and Paul, needless to say, regarded the experience as shot through with divine meaning, but they saw that meaning somewhat differently. For Luke its principal intention and effect was to make Paul aware of the fact that the Jesus whom he had been persecuting was really the Lord and Christ, thus changing the unbeliever and persecutor into the believer and preacher.

Paul also recognized in this experience the beginning of his Christian faith, but it is striking that he never refers to it in that connection. For him

---

[1]This can surely be said of each of the passages in which the appearance is being explicitly described. One must note, however, such vague or oblique allusions as "the Lord . . . appeared" in 9:17, "see the Just One" in 22:14, and "I have appeared to you" in 26:16. Perhaps Luke means that Christ "appeared" to Paul as a great and blinding light, but such would not be the kind of appearance of which Paul himself speaks.

its major significance lay in the fact that the experience made him a witness of the Resurrection and thus qualified him to be an apostle. He cites
it twice (1 Cor. 9:1; Gal. 1:11-17) as proof of his apostleship, and once (1
Cor. 15:8) as evidence for the Resurrection (but with secondary reference
to his apostleship, as the following verses show). But he never cites it as
the explanation (athough it was undoubtedly the occasion) of his Christian
faith and life. This particular way of conceiving of the meaning of the Damascus revelation is in line with what we have already observed of Paul's
reticence in speaking of ''visions and revelations of the Lord.'' The Christian life is the shared life of love, faith, and hope, which is the life of the
Spirit. No vision of the Lord is essentially a part of it. On the other hand,
the *apostle* (as distinguished from the ''man in Christ'') must be one who
has seen the Lord. Paul is not only the ''man in Christ,'' he is also an
''apostle of Jesus Christ.'' Hence the importance of this experience.

This word *apostle* was, in periods or areas at least, susceptible of two
interpretations. It could be used in a loose way to mean anyone ''sent out''
as an evangelist or missionary—it is regularly so used in the Didache, for
example. It appears that Paul also used it occasionally in this sense.[2] But
this is not his customary use of the term; in that use *apostle* always means
one who saw the Lord and was commissioned directly by him. Certainly
when Paul refers to himself as an apostle, he invariably has this higher
meaning in mind. Now it is noteworthy that Luke prefers to use the word
in the same limited sense. This meaning is clearly indicated as early as the
first chapter of Acts, where, having named the eleven apostles, the author
tells us that Peter raised the question with ''the brethren'' (about 120 of
them) as to who should take the twelfth, or Judas's place. He states the
qualifications of any nominee in the following words: ''One of the men
who has accompanied us during all the time that the Lord Jesus went in
and out among us, beginning from the baptism of John until the day when
he was taken up from us—one of these men must become with us a witness
to his resurrection.'' It is then described how Matthias was chosen to ''take
the place in this ministry and apostleship'' and how he ''was enrolled with
the eleven apostles.'' Throughout the book of Acts this way of using the
term *apostle* is consistently followed, although, as we shall see, the broader
use is not entirely lacking.

---

[2]Most clearly in 2 Cor. 8:23. Such passages as 1 Cor. 15:7 are ambiguous. But
see Phil. 2:25, where the word seems to have yet a third sense.

We have touched now upon a major difference between Paul's way of conceiving of himself and Luke's way of conceiving of him. Paul regards himself as being an apostle in this same high, limited sense, whereas Luke does not look upon Paul in that way. The only place in Acts where the word *apostle* is applied to Paul at all is in 14:4 and 14, and here the context strongly suggests the likelihood that the term is being used in the broad sense of "missionaries"—especially in view of the fact that Barnabas and he are mentioned together as "apostles." Paul in the book of Acts is, as Easton points out, an apostle "through man," if he is to be called an apostle at all.[3] In Acts 13:3 we read of his ordination to his office: "Then after fasting and prayer they laid their hands on them [Paul and Barnabas] and sent them off." Luke does not think of Paul as having been a witness of the Resurrection; rather he places in his mouth words that Paul himself would have repudiated with scorn: "God raised [Jesus] from the dead; and for many days he appeared to those who came up with him from Galilee to Jerusalem, who are now his witnesses to the people" (Acts 13:30-31). Indeed, is it not just this kind of interpretation of his apostleship, as resting upon the witness of others, that Paul *does* repudiate so vigorously and scornfully in the letter to the Galatians? We are not in the position of having to infer what Paul's enemies in Galatia—or at least some of them— were saying; Acts is actually saying the same thing a generation later.

We have only to compare the risen Jesus' appearances to his disciples as described or alluded to in Luke 24:13-Acts 1:6 with the vision of Paul in Acts 9:1-6 to see that Luke thinks of the latter as being of an entirely different order. Indeed, as we have already had occasion to observe, the interposition of the Ascension is enough to indicate Luke's understanding that appearances of the kind that could properly be thought of as bearing witness to the Resurrection were limited to the brief period of "forty days" (Acts 1:3) immediately following the Crucifixion. But Paul knows nothing of any Ascension—that is, as distinct from the Resurrection, which was itself exaltation (cf. Phil. 2:9)—and clearly implies that the appearance to him was of the same order as those to the other apostles (1 Cor. 15:3-9). He too was an apostle; he too had been a witness of the Resurrection; he too had seen the Lord.

---

[3]B. S. Easton, *Purpose of Acts* (London; S. P. C. K., 1926) 20. The reference is to Gal. 1:1.

III

The fact that in this passage, 1 Cor. 15:3-9, Paul quite obviously regards the appearances of the risen Jesus to his disciples as being in no way different in kind from his own experience of seeing the Lord is often cited as revealing the true character of the appearances to the other apostles. It also needs to be scrutinized, however, for the light it sheds upon the character of the appearance to Paul himself. When looked at from the first, or usual, point of view, the effect of Paul's words is to demonstrate the "spiritual" character of the appearances in the much later Gospels. The primitive Christian testimony to the fact of the Resurrection, making large use of the traditions of appearances to his disciples, was bound to encounter the objection that the evidence, if not faked, was dreamed. After all, it is notorious that we can see things that do not exist at all, and it is not unnatural that opponents and skeptics should take the line that the disciples of Jesus were the victims of such illusions. The inevitable effect of this kind of challenge was a tendency toward the materializing of the appearances; thus, in the Gospels and Acts, Jesus is represented as resuming his former life among his disciples, walking and talking with them, even eating with them. "See my hands and my feet," he says, "that it is I myself; handle me and see, for a spirit has not flesh and bones as you see that I have" (Luke 24:39). It is this resumption of a physical body that makes the Ascension necessary as a distinct event. For Jesus was actually known, within the experience of the early church, in the Spirit, not in the flesh. There must, then, have been a time when this radical passage from flesh to Spirit took place. If it did not occur at the moment of the Resurrection, a later moment must be found for it. That later moment was the Ascension; this is the conception of Matthew and John as well as Luke-Acts. But at the first it was not so: resurrection and exaltation were one event. Jesus was not raised to the earth and only later to the heavens. He was raised from the grave to the right hand of the throne of God; he passed directly from the fleshly life of earth to the spiritual life of heaven.[4] There can be

---

[4]It is interesting to observe that the Epistle to the Hebrews, although as late as the last decade of the first century, knows of no interval between resurrection and ascension. For this writer, as for Paul (and doubtless Mark), resurrection was exaltation. But whereas Paul more frequently calls this one event "the resurrection," the writer to the Hebrews characteristically thinks of it as the exaltation.

no doubt that Paul's contact with the risen Christ was of this completely spiritual or heavenly order, and when he places his experience in the same category with earlier appearances, as he does in 1 Cor. 15:3-9, he lets us know that they too were of this kind.

But, and this is not so generally noted or so easily stated, Paul also lets us know in that same passage something about the character of the appearance to *him*. In associating and classifying his experience with the earlier appearances, he separates it from later experiences of his own and of others. This separation must involve some recognition of a difference in kind as between the initial experiences of seeing the risen Christ, both the disciples' and his own, and "visions" of Christ that were still taking place. That such visions were continuing, at least for Paul, is indicated fairly clearly by his reference to "visions and revelations of the Lord" in 2 Cor. 12:1, together with the phrase in 12:7 "the abundance of revelations." Paul also refers to a revelation in Gal. 2:1 without indicating its content. Of course we may take "of the Lord" in 2 Cor. 12:1 as a genitive of source rather than an objective genitive (thus Goodspeed translates here "visions and revelations given me by the Lord"), but much the more natural sense is that Paul had visions from time to time of the Lord himself. Acts of course represents him as frequently subject to such experiences (18:9, 22:17; 23:11 [cf. 16:7], etc.), and Paul's own words fully support this representation.

But Paul seems to make a sharp distinction between these experiences and that "seeing" of the Lord to which he alludes in the three passages quoted at the beginning of this chapter. The former he hesitates to mention, as we have seen; the latter he affirms in the most matter-of-fact way. The former he regards as private; the latter as a fact of importance to the church. To speak of the former may seem to be boasting; to speak of the latter is to bear testimony to the resurrection of Christ. Paul cites only one appearance to him as evidence of this event. The isolation of this appearance cannot be accounted for simply on the ground that it was the first; he must have felt a difference in kind between it and the rest. That difference brought it into close connection with those earlier experiences of Jesus' disciples that he lists for us in 1 Cor. 15:3-9.

There is actually only one reference to the resurrection as such in Hebrews, but the idea of Christ's exaltation from the grave to the heavens is pervasive and of crucial importance to the argument of the book.

As to what this difference was we cannot know. If we could, we would know what made the experiences of the first witnesses so overwhelmingly convincing. Fortunately, we are not required to find an adequate psychological explanation; we know only that for some reason these experiences were absolutely indubitable and self-authenticating. Probably, on the human side, the difference lay in a feeling of complete matter-of-factness, as contrasted with the more ecstatic or visionary character of the later appearances. Certainly Luke sees a difference of this sort between the appearances to the "apostles" before the Ascension and the appearances to Paul afterward. Luke's terms in referring to Paul's experiences are ὅραμα (18:9), ἔκστασις (22:17) and ὀπτασία (26:19); he would not have used such terms to describe the pre-Ascension experiences of the disciples. Although Paul does not know the Ascension, he also apparently discriminates between earlier and later appearances. His manner of referring to these later appearances in 2 Cor. 12:2 suggests that the difference, as he too understood it, lay in this same more ecstatic character. Beyond this, however, we cannot go. Paul gives no hint of the concrete nature of his experience. Except that it was a "seeing" of Christ, and of Christ as both risen and exalted, he tells us nothing about it whatever. But Paul apparently regarded it as having been in kind unlike other visions he had had and as belonging with earlier experiences of other apostles, which could be taken as evidences of the Resurrection in a way the later visions could not be.

In a word, Paul's way of referring to his own experience in connection with the earlier resurrection appearances to Cephas, James and others will keep us, on the one hand, from accepting the suggestions of a physical, or almost physical, resurrection that are found in Matthew, John and Luke-Acts; but, on the other hand, it makes difficult our placing these experiences in the category of mere trances or visions. Paul was not only subject to such visions but also ready to recognize their supernatural origin and significance, yet he placed his initial seeing of the Lord in an altogether different category. Although coming long after the Resurrection had occurred, it made him a witness to that event and qualified him as "an apostle—not from men nor through man, but through Jesus Christ and God the Father, who raised him from the dead" (Gal. 1:1).

IV

Paul is quite sure that this revelation of Christ came to him not only suddenly and miraculously (as it did) but without psychological preparation of any kind. "For I would have you know, brethren," he writes, "that the gospel which was preached by me is not according to man. For I did not receive it from man, nor was I taught it, but it came through a revelation of Jesus Christ." As regards the negative part of this statement, however, we are justified in distrusting the accuracy even of Paul's own statement, although there is no question that it seemed true to him. The revelation of Christ in or near Damascus was not Paul's first contact with Christ. If it had been, the revelation could not have been self-authenticating and, therefore, could not have been revelation at all. How could Paul be so sure he had seen the Lord if he had not already in some sense come to know the Lord?

The fact that no persuasive answer to this question can be found leads some students of Paul to affirm that he must have been acquainted with Jesus before the Crucifixion. This is exceedingly unlikely. The only passage in Paul's letters that can be cited in support of it is 2 Cor. 5:16 ("Henceforth know we no man after the flesh; yea, though we have known Christ after the flesh, yet now henceforth know we him no more" [KJV]), and this passage is highly ambiguous. The Revised Standard Version renders it: "From now on, therefore, we regard no one from a human point of view; even though we once regarded Christ from a human point of view, we regard him thus no longer." If Paul had known Jesus, even at a distance, we would expect more in the way of allusion to so interesting and significant a circumstance than this one ambiguous clause.

And yet we cannot deny some previous knowledge of Christ on his part. Paul regarded himself as a witness of the Resurrection. The one who appeared to him was recognized to be the one who had lived and taught in Galilee and had been put to death in Jerusalem. That Paul had already a definite impression of this one is clearly indicated. And, it is important to note, the impression cannot have been simply a mental image of Jesus' physical form; it must have been an impression in the heart as well as in the mind—some "feeling" of the reality and quality of the personality of Jesus. Once we see that this is involved, we recognize that the whole question whether Paul ever saw Jesus in the flesh is largely irrelevant; for certainly he could not, in any case, have known Jesus well or intimately, and only such knowledge would account for the facts. Paul was certainly not a disciple of Jesus—or even a near disciple—and yet a disciple's understanding of, and attitude toward, Jesus seems to be presupposed by Paul's recognition of, and response to, the one who appeared to him.

We touch here upon one of the profoundest meanings of the Resurrection. This meaning is the presence in the community of believers of a *living memory* of Jesus. This means, not a memory, however sharp and vivid, in the minds and hearts of individual disciples, but rather a shared remembrance, alive and growing, and not less true, but rather more deeply true, on that account. Papias at the middle of the second century speaks of it as "the living voice." That voice began to speak from the moment of the Resurrection, and it speaks still. This memory of Jesus has its unique character because it is a memory not of one who was, but of one who is. The one who is remembered is still known; the one who is known is also remembered. To remember Jesus in just the way the community remembered him was also to know him as living Lord; to enter into a knowledge of his present reality and lordship in the life of the community was to enter also into the memory of him. This fact is not subject to adequate psychological explanation, nor is it comparable with any other. It is both unique and inexplicable, but indubitable. It is indeed the meaning of the Resurrection.

For the empirical basis of faith in the Resurrection of Christ is nothing less, or more, than this realized continuity between past and present—between the one remembered as the human master and friend and the one now known as the divine Spirit of the fellowship. This continuity was not a conclusion from the Resurrection; on the contrary, the Resurrection (if conceived as a momentary incident in time and place) was itself an inference from the known, self-authenticating character of this continuity. Since the one who was now known as the Lord and Spirit within the fellowship was he who had been crucified, he must have risen from the dead. We have spoken in these chapters of "witnesses of the Resurrection." But in the strict sense there were no witnesses of the Resurrection. Not even the latest parts of the New Testament contain any account of the incident itself. Men and women see Christ after he arose, and they see the empty tomb in which he lay—but the Resurrection itself they do not see. With instinctive reticence not only the Gospel writers but, for the most part, even the later legend makers leave that crucial moment in the mystery where it has always been and must always be. We do not know what happened; we know only that he who lives in our midst is he who suffered death upon the cross.

This identity of the crucified Jesus with the living Christ was not established by any argument. It was not "proved" to anyone. It was something given within the life of the community. It was indeed the essential character of the community, the distinctive principle of its life. This means that it was the Spirit. Every living community has its spirit; the important thing about the church was that its spirit was the Holy Spirit—a spirit not created from within but given from above. This Spirit was received as the very presence of Christ, and his coming was the effective "proof" of the Resurrection. In Acts 5:32 Peter says as much: "And we are witnesses to these things [that is, to the fact of Jesus' resurrection], and so is the Holy Spirit whom God has given to those who obey him." The appearances in visual form of Christ, whatever the concrete nature of these experiences or their psychological character, were only an accompaniment, however indispensable in the providence of God, of the essential event, which was the coming of the Spirit and thus the coming into being of the community in whose life Christ lives still. And when the Spirit came, not only was the risen Christ known as an indubitable, present reality, but also the memory of the man Jesus came alive with a new vitality and a new meaning. The author of the Fourth Gospel is profoundly true to the experience of the church when he has Jesus say, "But . . . the Holy Spirit, whom the Father will send in my name, he will teach you all things, and bring to your remembrance all that I have said to you" (14:26).

Returning now to Paul, we see that any contact he had with the primitive community that was more than merely external or mechanical was also contact with Christ—and with Christ not only as known and worshiped but also as remembered, for the two were indissolubly one. Christ had begun to make himself known to Paul—perhaps against the latter's will—as the Spirit of the persecuted *koinonia* before he made himself known in the visual experience in which Paul's conversion culminated. Otherwise, Paul would not have been able to interpret the visual experience as he did, if indeed it could have occurred at all. The same thing is true of the experiences of Cephas, the Twelve, the five hundred and the rest. For them, too, the visual manifestations, whatever their character, were the consequence of the Spirit's coming and were given their meaning by the Spirit. To be sure, Luke, who sees an interval between the Resurrection and the Ascension, regards the coming of the Spirit and thus the creation of the church as being also a distinct and later event. But in the beginning it was not so: the Resurrection, the Exaltation, the coming of the Spirit, the coming into being of the church were different ways of conceiving and describing the central moment in which the meaning of the whole event of Jesus Christ was revealed and fulfilled.

The appearances to Paul and to the others were the accompaniment of that moment, not essential parts of it. They represent the visualization of what was already a reality in the life of the community. They served the indispensable function of making more vividly realizable what was already true and at least dimly known—the presence of Christ, alive after his passion, in the midst of his own.

Chapter VIII

The New Creation

Near the beginning of the preceding chapter, a summary of Paul's meaning when he speaks of himself as "a man in Christ" was proposed in the following terms: he refers to the fact that he has, by God's mercy, been made a part of that ultimate, eschatological order, that divine community of love, which in the Gospels is called the kingdom of God and which is already proleptically and partially present among us as the church, whose spirit (that is, the inner principle that constitutes and distinguishes it as a living community) authenticates itself both as the Spirit of God and as the continuing reality and presence of Christ. The meaning and limits of this suggested equivalence among the terms "kingdom of God," "Christ," "Spirit," "love," "community" and "church" obviously need to be more carefully defined, and this chapter will be concerned with that undertaking.

At the outset it is important to recognize that we are not dealing here with a series of logically related ideas, but with the actual stuff of Paul's religious life. Any discussion of these terms is bound to take them up in a certain order and, therefore, is constantly in danger of suggesting that they stand in a certain logical or chronological relation, one idea implying another or one experience leading to another. But the whole point in using the word *equivalence* is to suggest that the several terms are various ways of designating *one* experience. There is significance in this variety—that is, the various terms serve to bring out various aspects or suggest various theological implications of the one experience. But the experience is *one*, and the terms are primarily empirical terms. Certainly it is as such that we are primarily concerned with them, since our first intention is to consider, not the categories of the theologian, but the life of the man himself.

I

We may most appropriately begin with "Jesus Christ" (with which belong "Christ," "the Lord Jesus Christ," and usually, "the Lord") as being the most inclusive of the several terms and as coming nearest to suggesting the whole range of empirical meaning that Paul is seeking to express and to share with his readers. No one who so much as glances through Paul's letters can fail to note how constantly the term appears (a rough count would indicate something like two and one-half times per page in a correspondence that runs to 110 pages), and in what varied contexts. Virtually all the prepositions are required to express the relationship in which Paul thinks of himself, and believers generally, as standing to Christ: we find again and again "for Christ" and "because of Christ," "through Christ," "by Christ," "with Christ," "to Christ," "of Christ" and, most frequently perhaps, "in Christ." The number and range of these prepositional phrases are enough to suggest the richness and complexity of the meaning of the term. Paul sums it up when he says, "For to me to live *is* Christ" (Phil. 1:21).

Elsewhere I have ventured to use the words *person, event* and *community* in seeking to analyze this meaning, at the same time insisting that, as in the case of the doctrine of the Trinity itself, with which this trichotomy has a certain correspondence, "these three are one."[1] Of these, the most simple and obvious is the person: and, as we should expect, the word *Christ* is most frequently used in that sense. Paul knows himself to belong to that person; he is Christ's slave. In devotion to him Paul finds the whole meaning of his life.

This person is, as we were reminding ourselves at the end of the preceding chapter, both remembered and still known. He is both the man of Galilee, which he was, and the man of heaven, which he is. The essential meaning of the Resurrection lies in the fact of this identity. The Jesus who died is the Christ who is alive forevermore—such was the earliest Christian confession, "Jesus is Lord." One is bound to note here, however, a slight difference of emphasis as between Paul and the more primitive

---

[1]John Knox, *On the Meaning of Christ* (New York: Scribner's, 1947) 19ff., et passim; *Jesus, Lord and Christ* (New York: Harper, 1958) 206ff.

church—probably as between him and many of his contemporaries. Paul's
thought about Christ the person always moves from the "Christ who lives"
to the "Jesus who died," always from the one known to the one remembered. It is the present living reality that comes first to his mind when he
speaks of Christ. That may well have been true also of Peter and of others
who had known Jesus in the flesh, but surely not in quite the same sense
or degree. The wonder of the Resurrection to these men and women would
consist of the fact that he whom they had known in intimate human intercourse, and whose death they had witnessed, was indeed alive and was
known to them in even more intimate fellowship. The wonder of the Resurrection to Paul consisted of the fact that this one whom he now knew as
Lord had actually suffered death upon the cross. They speak of "Jesus
whom God raised up"; Paul speaks of "Christ and him crucified."

At first sight this last phrase seems to leave out the Resurrection entirely. But it seems to do so only because we suppose Paul's thought was
moving, as ours customarily does, in a forward direction. When *we* read
the phrase "Christ and him crucified," we think first of the human Jesus,
of his life of devotion and service, and our minds then move forward to the
cross. But when Paul wrote the phrase, he was thinking first of all of the
risen, exalted Christ, and his thought moved *backward* to the cross. Perhaps this fact partly explains the paucity of allusions to Jesus' earthly life
in Paul's letters. His attention, as it moves backward, is arrested by the
Crucifixion, which itself epitomizes so perfectly the theological significance and the moral character of the whole earthly life that he does not look
beyond it. Having begun, so to speak, from the end of the book, he has
already reached the climax of the story. Thus, far from omitting reference
to the Resurrection, Paul's phrase takes its start from it; the word *Christ*
means primarily the one now known as living and present Lord. The same
sequence of thought—from the present, or even the future, to the past—is
indicated in many scores of passages: for example, "It is no longer I who
live, but Christ who lives in me . . . who loved me and gave himself for
me" (Gal. 2:20), or "That I may know him and the power of his resurrection, and may share his sufferings, becoming like him in his death"
(Phil. 3:10). The words "the life of Christ" mean for us the career of Jesus
of Nazareth, but for Paul they would have meant something quite different—the present reality and lordship of the risen one. So, indeed, he actually uses an equivalent phrase in Rom. 5:10: "For if while we were
enemies we were reconciled to God by the death of his Son, much more,

now that we are reconciled, shall we be saved by his life." The "life of Christ" is not the remembered life that preceded his death, but the life that followed it—the present life of the Son of God.

This present life of the Son of God was for Paul more than a fact believed. It was a reality known. To be sure, Paul speaks constantly of "having faith" in Christ; but faith, as Paul uses the word, does not mean mere assent to a statement as true in the way one believes a fact of history or geography. Faith is not the intellectual acceptance of an abstract truth: it is the full personal reception and appropriation of a concrete personal reality. Paul would never have set faith over against knowledge in the way we often do. If by knowledge is meant our immediate grasp or apprehension of an actual object, faith *is* the knowledge of Christ. If Paul had made a distinction, as we sometimes do, between the things he *knew* and the things he "only believed," then undoubtedly the present reality of Christ would have been found among the things he knew. But Paul does not use the words *faith* and *knowledge* in this way. To know Christ, in the later Johannine sense, is to have faith in him; to have faith in him is to know him. This empirical meaning of the word *faith* appears unmistakably and constantly in his letters. A good illustration lies at hand in the passage from Galatians just quoted in another connection. After saying, "It is no longer I who live, but Christ who lives in me," Paul continues, "and the life I now live in the flesh I live by faith in the Son of God." Here "faith in the Son of God" is fully equated with the actual realized presence of that Son of God— "Christ who lives in me." In the same way he can refer to "Christ in you" (Col. 1:27). This actual empirical knowledge of Christ as alive after his passion is, as we have seen (pp. 104-105), the essential meaning and the unassailable ground of the resurrection faith.

II

But to set forth adequately Paul's experience of Christ, it is not enough to say that Christ is the person remembered in the flesh and now known in the Spirit; we must also say that this person is the Messiah. And to say that is to say something about the "event" and the "community"; for the Messiah is most significant, not for what he is in himself, but for what he does, or rather for what God does through him. Thus, when Paul affirms the Jesus whom he knows as Master and Lord to be "Jesus Christ," he is affirming that through him God has acted, or is acting, for our ultimate salvation—that is, for salvation from *all* our enemies, including the sin that

divides us and the death that destroys us—and that through him the ultimate order of righteousness, love and life, the kingdom of God, has been
granted us. This act of God on our behalf, to be sure, has not been consummated; this consummation will come only when Christ returns. But it
has been decisively accomplished; sin and death have been defeated and
judged, and their final destruction, soon to take place, will be merely the
execution of a sentence already pronounced. The kingdom of God is still
to be fully revealed; but it is already won for us and guaranteed to us, and
we wait only for the moment, soon to come, when what has already been
awarded to us shall become our actual and complete possession.

Such a statement is bound to suggest two questions: How does Paul
know that Jesus is the Messiah, that he has won for us the kingdom of God?
And, how does Paul interpret or picture Christ's messianic work? In answer to the second of these questions it must be said that Paul has various
and not always consistent ways of explaining just how Christ has fulfilled
the office of the Messiah. His explanation, as is frequently said, seized on
any possible metaphor suggested by his environment and used any terms
made available to him by contemporary thought patterns, Jewish and Hellenistic. Thus, Christ is represented as paying our ransom, or as offering
the sufficient sacrifice for our sin, or as winning a victory over the demonic enemies who through Adam's disobedience got us in thrall. Paul
does not think of these representations of the work of Christ as mere met-
aphors. So congenial and integral to his mind is the apocalypticism of his
period that when he speaks of Christ's victory over sin and death, he is
speaking with the starkest realism—that is, sin and death are actual, almost personal, powers Christ has defeated. But it is almost as clear that
when he explains Christ's death as having been, in some sense, the pay-
ment of a debt or penalty, an act of obedience and devotion offered to God
on our behalf that made possible the righteous God's acquitting sinners,
he is speaking no less realistically. Modern writers sometimes try hard to
relieve Paul of any serious belief that Christ's death had this kind of significance, but they do not succeed. Such passages as Rom. 3:24-26 and
5:6-11 clearly point the other way. We simply cannot take Paul's allusions
to Christ's vicarious satisfaction of God's demands any more than his references to Christ's defeat of our demonic adversaries as being mere metaphor. But whatever difficulties we may have in obtaining a clear view of
how the humble life of Jesus, his death and his resurrection could have had
this saving effect, it is the effect itself that is important, and to it Paul bears

consistent testimony in every paragraph we have from his hand. That effect is membership—open to any who will in humility and faith accept it—in the ultimate, the heavenly, order of righteousness and peace, of reconciliation and atonement, of Spirit and life, which is the kingdom of God.

Jesus, then, is not simply the person; he is the representative and embodiment of a new kind of humanity, a humanity free from sin and from all threat of corruption and death. He, like Adam, represents an entire order of creation; he is the "second man." To know the risen Christ is to be made a participant in a whole new realm of the Spirit. To belong to Christ is to belong to a new, redeemed humanity. The most frequent meaning of the phrase "in Christ" appears in the statement, "As in Adam all die, so also in Christ shall all be made alive" (1 Cor. 15:22). As natural human beings we are "in Adam"; as such we sin and die. But already we may be "in Christ" and thus share in a new and endless life: "Death is swallowed up in victory."

Paul knows, of course, that the full meaning of this victory cannot be realized within history. The order of pure love and of full and endless life, if it should enter into history, would by its very coming destroy history: "Flesh and blood cannot inherit the kingdom of God" (1 Cor. 15:50). It is for this reason that Paul usually speaks of salvation as being in the future and says in effect over and over again, "In hope we are saved." But this hope (and here we come to our second question: How can Paul *know* that Jesus is the Messiah?) is not mere hope; it is hope already beginning to be realized. Christ is not merely to come; he has come. His victory is not merely expected; it has been won. The kingdom of God, the realm of the Spirit, is not simply an object of eager longing or of expectation, however confident; the whole ground of the Christian life lies in the fact that in the church the kingdom of God is really, though partially, present, and that in the Spirit, which has already been given, we have a foretaste, an advance installment, of the whole eschatological order of the Spirit.

III

Paul does not often use the word *church* except in designating particular local groups, but the reality of the church in a more general, or truly catholic, sense is presupposed in every word he writes. The author of the Epistle to the Ephesians understands this and, at this point at least, only makes explicit what Paul is constantly taking for granted. The church is, as was just now suggested, the immediate ground of one's life as a Chris-

tian—the basis, not only of one's conviction as to the significance of the
past (that is, of what has been done through Christ) and of one's hope for
the future (that is, for the ultimate redemption from sin and death), but also
of one's actual present existence as a Christian. As a Jew, Paul shared in
the corporate life of Judaism; that is what it meant to be a Jew. Now, although he does not think of himself as ceasing to be a Jew, he finds himself
a member of a new people—new because it has a new spirit and is open to
all of every nation simply on the condition of faith, and yet old since it is
Israel become itself, the fulfillment of God's ancient promises. But whether
as Jew or Christian, for Paul the religious life is life within the religious
community. By "life" Paul would not mean merely a "way of living"—
whether ethical or cultic—although the life of a religious community will
inevitably express itself in characteristic patterns of thought and conduct.
He would mean something more profound and more dynamic, something
nearer the original meaning of the word "life." By the "life of the church"
he would mean the essential vitality of the church, that which makes it an
integral, distinctive and living body, the inner constitutive organic principle, as mysterious and undefinable in a living society as in a living plant,
and yet as undeniable. To be a Christian is to share in that corporate life.

This new community was God's new creation. It can be said, of course,
that every living thing is God's creation, although Paul was not as vividly
aware of this fact as we may wish he had been. An esteemed teacher of
mine, Henry Nelson Wieman, used to say, "Man makes mechanisms; God
makes organisms." That may be too neat a statement to be true—and I am
not sure I have quoted Wieman exactly—but it points to the truth. Life is
always God's gift. The familiar poet is right, of course, in saying that "only
God can make a tree"; but he is wrong in saying that a poem—that is, a
living poem—can be made by a fool (although perhaps a fool can come
nearer to making one than a wise man can). Still, only God can make a
living poem, or a living friendship, or a living community, or any other
living thing. We can put things together, and our part in the creative process is therefore important, because it is necessary that things be put together, and any ingenuity we may develop in putting the right things
together in the right proportions and relations is all to the good. It is good
to place the best seed in the best soil. But once this is done, God must create the living plant. So, also, two persons in love wonder at what has happened to them in just the same way as Tennyson wonders at the flower in
the crannied wall. "This is the Lord's doing: it is marvelous in our eyes."

All living things make themselves known to the sensitive and discerning as being, not human construction, but God's creation.

But the church, the living community into which Paul found himself incorporated, made itself known as God's creation in a peculiar sense. It was his *new* creation. In the event of which Jesus' life, death and resurrection were the center God had spoken, not simply in the way he was always speaking through nature or through historical developments or crises, but in a way as unprecedented and decisive as when in the beginning he said, "Let there be light." It was the eschatological event, comparable in importance only with the original creative moment. As a consequence of it, we are no longer in the position of merely expecting the kingdom of God. In the event that culminated in the creation of the new community not only is the eternal reality of God's kingdom disclosed to us, but it has itself become proleptically—even if partially and imperfectly—present and dynamic within history. To belong to this community in truth is to "walk in newness of life"—to taste, at least, the quality of the life of heaven. Paul does not discuss the question, later to be debated, of the relation of the church to the kingdom of God, but he might have said something like this: In complete actuality the church is most certainly not the kingdom of God; it belongs to history, suffers from all the vicissitudes of historical existence, and shares in all the limitations and sins that are our natural lot: but in inner principle it *is* the kingdom, for the source of its distinctive character is its actual participation in the event toward which all creation has been moving. The church is the church because it belongs, not to this age, but to the age that is to come and in Christ has already begun to be. The church, in the truest and most authentic sense, *is* the kingdom of God insofar as that kingdom has been able to find room within the present world.

Paul uses once a very striking metaphor to express his understanding of the essential nature of the church. He says in Phil. 3:20, "But we are a colony of heaven." This is Moffatt's translation of a Greek text that, rendered more literally, says, "Our commonwealth is in heaven"; but the meaning is the same. Perhaps it is not an accident that it was a native of the British Isles who saw the appropriateness of the word *colony*. What is the relation of a colony to the home country? It is probably separated from it by many thousands of miles. Conditions of climate and topography are likely to be quite different. It finds itself surrounded by, and in a measure participating in, ways of living that are foreign to the life of the home country. And yet in the deepest, truest sense it is not only closely related to the homeland, it *is* the homeland. The English colony, in the original meaning of the terms, was not simply bound to England; it was itself a transplanted England. This is to say that, however far from England it might be in space and time, and whatever else of England it might lack, the *spirit* of England was present in it.

And so we are led back again to Paul's doctrine of the Spirit.

IV

The distinctive, decisively identifying thing about the church, as of any human community, is its spirit; and the spirit of the church, like the spirit of a colony, is not indigenous. It is the spirit of another country and another age, of heaven and the kingdom of God. It is the spirit of the ultimate, the eschatological order, miraculously present within history. It is thus the presence of God himself, the Holy Spirit, God's own Spirit. So Paul often designates it. But this same Spirit may also be called the Spirit of Christ, for the coming of the Spirit is the culmination of the whole event, Jesus Christ. The Spirit came into our world with him, just as—and these two are the same—the church came into being with him. Moreover, as we have already noted more than once, this Spirit makes itself known as his very presence and is thus itself the reality of the Resurrection. Thus Paul can speak of the Spirit, which constitutes and distinguishes the church, as being not only the Spirit of God or the Spirit of Christ (as the context may make appropriate or desirable) but the very Christ himself.

This Spirit is the divine reality of the church's life. It is the bond that not only binds the church with heaven and thus distinguishes it but also binds its members together and thus unites it. The Spirit is the community, or *koinonia,* in which the church essentially consists. The true unity of the church is the "communion of the Holy Spirit"—a unity not to be imposed from above, or indeed to be imposed at all, since it is already there. Where the Spirit is, there is the church; where the church is, there is the Spirit. We can produce neither the one nor the other; both are God's gift to all who will receive the Christ in humility and faith.

For the Spirit is also love, that particular kind of love for which the New Testament had to find a new word, *agape,* the love that made itself known in Jesus, seemed to find perfect and inevitable expression in the Cross, and became the living breath of the new creation. If the *koinonia* of the church is the *koinonia* of the Spirit, it is also the *koinonia* of *agape.* For *love,* in Paul at least, never means primarily an ethical attitude (although such an attitude is always implied or involved); it means a concrete living, spiritual reality. Love is always the love of God; and this love is the dynamic, outgoing reality of God himself, reaching to us, redeeming us, possessing us, using us. In other words, the love of God is the presence or Spirit of God. It is on this account that agape is greater than faith or hope. Faith is our way of receiving God's gift, and hope is a consequence of our receiving it, but love is the gift itself.

All of this is now "in part." What has been said of the church is fully true only of the kingdom of God; what has been said of the Spirit is fully true only of the coming age; what has been said of *koinonia* and *agape* is fully true only in heaven. But the church is a colony of heaven; the Spirit is an advance installment of our inheritance; the love we are given to know is also the ground of a sure hope; and the life we now have in Christ contains in itself the promise of an ultimate redemption.

So much for an effort to interpret Paul's conception of the objective reality in which he knows himself to be incorporated, and which he usually calls by Christ's name. Let us now turn to the more subjective side: What is the meaning for the individual of this life within the new creation? What does it mean to live "in Christ"? We have not been able to avoid this topic completely in this chapter, especially in the final paragraphs; but we may now consider it somewhat more fully.

Chapter IX

The Life in Christ

We have seen that to be "in Christ" meant to Paul to stand within that new order of relationships which God brought into being in connection with Jesus and, in some way defying adequate or exact explanation, through the instrumentality of his death and life. To be "in Christ" was to be an organic part of the new creation, of which the risen Christ was the supreme manifestation and the effective symbol; it was, indeed, to belong to the eschatological kingdom of God that had already appeared within history as the church. But as we have also seen, Paul could not speak of participation in this corporate reality without speaking also of the Spirit and of *agape* and, therefore, of the quality and significance of the new life itself as it was realized within his own experience as a believer. This new life made itself known to him as forgiveness and emancipation, as pardon from the guilt of sin and release from its power, or to use Paul's words, as *justification* (with which "reconciliation" is closely connected) and *redemption*. The meaning of neither the one nor the other of these two elements in the new life, it must always be remembered, could be fully known within the present age. Both were primarily and essentially eschatological realities, as was the new life itself. But just as *agape* and Spirit had been truly, even if only partially, given, so forgiveness and deliverance from the power of sin had been truly, even if only partially, received. With these two aspects of the new life *as received* we shall now be concerned.

I

It may at first seem strange and arbitrary to ascribe such great importance to forgiveness in the experience of Paul, in view of the fact that he so seldom uses the term. Indeed, it is not altogether clear or sure that he uses the noun at all. It occurs once in Ephesians (1:7), which Paul almost certainly did not write, once in Colossians (1:14), which is the most dubious of the other letters, and nowhere else in the Pauline epistles. As for the verb *forgive*, Paul employs it several times in 2 Corinthians and in Col. 3:13 (χαρίζεσθαι) in discussing how we shall deal with others. But only twice in all his letters does he speak of God as "forgiving" us; and of these, one instance occurs in Colossians (2:13—again χαρίζεσθαι) and the other in a quotation from the Old Testament in Rom. 4:7 (ἀφιέναι).[1] Equally striking is the absence of any emphasis upon the idea of "repentance" in Paul's letters. He uses this term—noun and verb—as seldom as the other; the references he makes to repenting of wrongdoing (Rom. 2:4; 2 Cor. 7:9-10; 12:21) are never such as to make it a condition of salvation or to bring it into important or integral relation with the new life. Given his disuse of the term *forgiveness,* this is to be expected, for repentance and forgiveness obviously belong together as two sides of a single shield. Only the penitent can, in the nature of the case, *receive* forgiveness; and upon the penitent only, in the nature of the case, can even God bestow it.

The absence of any emphasis whatever in Paul's letters upon these two concepts is much more than interesting or even curious—it is nothing short of astounding. This is true, first of all, because nothing in Paul's religious background, as we are able to know it, prepares us to expect it. Although, as we have seen, there is good reason to doubt Paul's education under Gamaliel (see p. 21), we cannot deny to him considerable knowledge of rabbinical theology; and stress upon the necessity and appropriateness of repentance, as well as upon God's willingness to forgive, was a constant feature of rabbinical teaching. Because Paul seems to represent Judaism as lacking these ideas, it has been held by many that he could not have been a pupil of the rabbis at all (so Montefiore and others); but more important as an argument against his having had rabbinical training than Paul's alleged misrepresentation of rabbinism is his own disuse of these same ideas of forgiveness and repentance. However, this feature cannot be explained

---

[1]But note Eph. 4:32 and a reference to Christ's forgiving us in Col. 3:13.

by any theory of exposure or nonexposure to any particular form of teaching within Judaism, for the idea of God's being ready to forgive the penitent is characteristic of the Old Testament itself, especially of those parts of it—the Prophets and the Psalms—with which Paul shows himself to have been best acquainted, and which he found most congenial. And yet Paul quotes only one Old Testament passage containing a reference to God's forgiveness (from Ps. 32:1-2)—

> Blessed are those whose iniquities are forgiven,
>   and whose whose sins are covered;
> blessed is the man against whom the Lord
>   will not reckon his sin;

and his discussion of even this passage makes no use whatever of the term *forgiveness,* the attention being focused entirely upon the second of the two parallel ideas, the blessedness of "the man to whom God reckons righteousness apart from works" (Rom. 4:2-10).

But if Paul's neglect of many Old Testament passages is surprising, how shall we describe his apparent disregard of what is undoubtedly the most characteristic, constant and pervasive feature of Jesus' own teaching? According to the Gospel of Mark, Jesus began his work with a call to repentance and a promise of salvation, and the Gospels make abundantly clear that God's forgiveness was at the very heart of this redemption. We are to forgive others because God is always ready to forgive us, and unless we forgive others God cannot forgive us. All restrictions upon forgiveness—upon God's as a fact or upon ours as a duty—are swept away: given repentance, the kind of forgiveness God offers to us and requires of us knows no limit and is subject to no condition. Jesus seems often to have assured individuals of God's forgiveness, and his whole ministry, under one of its most important aspects, might be described as a commentary on the Old Testament text:

> The sacrifices of God are a broken spirit:
> A broken and a contrite heart, O God, thou wilt not despise.

To the meek, to the poor in spirit, to those who hunger and thirst after righteousness, Jesus promised the comfort and mercy of God. He tells us that he came to call sinners to repentance and warns that unless we "turn and become like children," we shall not see the kingdom of heaven. He speaks of the "joy before the angels of God over one sinner who repents"; and in some of his parables (notably those of the prodigal son and of the publican and the Pharisee in the temple) he sets forth the concrete meaning of both penitence and forgiveness and of their close and essential interrelation in images of supreme power and beauty. Paul, as we have seen, shares in the corporate memory of this man. How could he have failed to make use of ideas so conspicuously present in Jesus' teachings and so suggestive of the whole character and quality of Jesus' life itself?

But what makes Paul's disuse of these terms most amazing of all is not such facts as these about his religious background but rather the fact that Paul himself so manifestly knows the realities to which these terms apply. If any reader of Paul's letters were asked to name the important and characteristic features of Paul's way of understanding the meaning of the gospel, he or she would be certain to include these two features, whatever else might be added or omitted: (a) Paul's vivid sense of being, along with all others, a sinner before God—guilty of transgressions against God's holy law for which he cannot properly atone—and (b) Paul's knowledge that God has shown mercy toward us, freeing us from the guilt of our sins and reconciling us to himself. No word occurs more constantly in Paul's letters that ''grace'' (χάρις). Grace means God's favor toward those who do not deserve it—a favor, indeed, whose reality can be known and whose benefits can be received only by those who *know* that they do not deserve it. The *substance* of repentance and forgiveness is surely here. Indeed, some scholars see in the presence in Luke's Gospel alone of such parables of Jesus as those of the prodigal son and Pharisee and the publican an indication of special Pauline influence upon the author, so close and congenial such stories are to Paul's characteristic way of feeling and understanding the religious life. It would be disciples of Paul, these scholars hold, who felt most keenly the truth and significance of this particular strain in the gospel tradition. Whether we find this suggestion altogether convincing or not will depend somewhat upon how important and authentic we believe the idea of salvation by God's mercy rather than by our merit to have been in Jesus' own teaching. I happen to be one who believes that this idea was for him central, decisive and constant, and that Paul in his characteristic emphasis upon redemption rather than attainment, upon grace rather than works, is only following where Jesus has led the way. But such an observation serves only to make more remarkable the fact that Paul, knowing so well the reality of repentance and forgiveness, makes so little use of those terms. Let us turn to a discussion of the terms Paul does use.

II

The place of forgiveness is taken in Paul by two terms, *justification* and *reconciliation*. "Justification" is essentially a legal term and means "acquittal." "Reconciliation" is essentially a personal term and means the restoration of community. Now of these terms the one that applies most immediately and directly to our felt need is "reconciliation," for according to Paul's diagnosis, the fundamentally wrong thing about humanity and history is estrangement—enmity and division between human beings and their Creator, which means enmity and division between the individual and his or her neighbor, and enmity and division within the individual's own soul. What we most need, therefore, is reconciliation—the community we were considering in the preceding chapter. But our estrangement is the consequence of sin, which under one of its aspects is humanity's transgression of God's law. No reconciling process that bypassed this moral fact could be effective. Reconciliation between human beings and God, as indeed any reconciliation between persons, is possible only on a basis of righteousness and truth. The creation of this basis of righteousness and truth is what Paul calls "justification." He does not think of justification and reconciliation as being actually separate—it would be as inconceivable that one should be justified without also being reconciled as that one should be reconciled without having been justified—but they do represent distinct phases of God's saving act. "Since we are justified by faith, we have peace with God" (Rom. 5:1). We must be acquitted; only so can the holy God enter into fellowship with us and we with him.

Now it is clear that with these two terms Paul is seeking to represent the meaning of forgiveness. For what is forgiveness but reconciliation on the basis of righteousness and truth? Forgiveness is not mere justification; it is not a state of acquitting or being acquitted; it has no place in a court of law. Forgiveness is the restoration of a personal relationship, whether between individuals or between human beings and God (and these two are truly one). But this personal relationship—this community—cannot be restored or sustained through the ignoring or the mere forgetting of the wrong that destroyed it. The wrong must be acknowledged and in some way dealt with. We have a way of saying "forgive and forget," as though forgetting represented the ultimate meaning of forgiving. But we do not forgive by merely forgetting, and certainly we are not forgiven that way. To forgive or to be forgiven, even among ourselves, if we have greatly wronged another or have been greatly wronged, is one of the profoundest experiences of reality it is given to us to have. A wrong, done or suffered, ceases to be divisive and destructive, not when it is forgotten by each person separately, but when it is remembered by both persons together. When two persons, the wronged and the wrongdoer, can remember the wrong together in the same way and as a shared experience, then, and only then, is it truly forgiven. The wrong thing must be completely accepted for what it is and must be appropriately handled. Forgiveness is not a closing of one's eyes. Such indulgence of another, or of oneself, if it concerns anything important, is weakness and illusion; forgiveness is always strength and truth.

When Paul speaks of justification and reconciliation, therefore, he is distinguishing elements that actually belong to the meaning of God's forgiveness of us. We might argue that his neglect of the term *forgiveness* itself involves no loss—indeed, means gain, since his analysis prevents our ignoring either element in its meaning, either the justice in it or the mercy. The fact and importance of this gain should be gratefully recognized; nevertheless, it must be said that the division that Paul made in the meaning of forgiveness was one of the most tragically fateful developments in the whole history of Christian theology and, therefore, in the intellectual history of the West. For although both justice and mercy are in forgiveness, they are there *together* —not simply combined and therefore separable, but united indissolubly. The justice is not mere justice, and the mercy is not mere mercy; each is modified by the other so as to make a mercy that is also just and a justice that is also merciful. When we say that God *forgives,* we are saying that *this* is the character of *his* justice and of *his* mercy. But Paul by dividing forgiveness into two parts opened the way to division in the nature of God himself; his justice is seen as mere justice and his mercy as only mercy. He is the just Judge and the merciful Father; he is not, as he is for Jesus, a Father who is both just and merciful—truly (that is, appropriately) just only because he is also merciful, truly (that is, authentically) merciful only because he is also just. We must not fail to note that this dichotomy in Paul's view of God is far from complete or consistent: it is God's *grace* alone that makes possible our justification as well as our reconciliation; it is God who by offering his own Son in love provides the basis for our acquittal. But division within the character of God and within his reconciling act, while by no means complete (as it later became in Marcionism), is nevertheless undeniably present. And this division is not supported either by the teaching of Jesus or by the church's experience of the forgiveness of God in Christ—experience that immeasurably deepens for us the meaning of forgiveness but does not modify its essential structure as Jesus' teaching sets it forth.

For, as a matter of empirical fact, there is no moral contradiction in forgiveness that has to be resolved by some theory of compensating or appeasing or justifying atonement. No matter how grievously we may have wronged, or have been wronged by, another, we are not aware of any sacrifice of righteousness and truth in the experience of forgiving or being forgiven. On the contrary, if forgiveness is forgiveness (and not mere indulgence), we know truth and righteousness to have been vindicated and to have been established as the very basis of the renewed relationship. No reader of Jesus' parable of the prodigal son who knows the meaning of forgiveness will feel the slightest moral protest against the father's way of welcoming back the son who had "devoured [his] living with harlots." We are not likely to object that the father should have asked some compensation or imposed some penalty, that otherwise his moral integrity or the moral integrity of the family has been violated. The elder brother felt so, to be sure; but the father did not, the younger son did not, and quite clearly, Jesus did not. Neither do we; we know that the father in that story acted in just the appropriate way, that there is a justice that belongs to the family as certainly as there is another kind of justice that belongs to the law court, and that the justice of the father, while not of the sort that would be appropriate or even legitimate in a court of law or a market (represented in this story by the elder son), is nevertheless authentic justice. And can it be seriously argued that in this parable Jesus is thinking merely about human relationships—that he is not intending to say something about the nature of God and of his dealings with us? Must he not be telling us that in what we know best and most intimately, the life of the home, the meaning of the mystery of the kingdom of God lies hidden, and revealed?

In such a view, the thing that preserves the moral character of forgiveness, keeps it from degenerating into a weak and false indulgence, is not a penalty paid or an expiatory act performed, either by the offender or by another vicariously on his or her behalf, but rather *repentance* . Repentance is necessary, but repentance is all God asks. Of course it would not be all if God were not love, just as it would not be necessary if God were not also truth. Repentance, however, is no small or easy thing; it is an act of realization so radical and costly that only God's grace can move us to it or make us capable of it. For just as forgiveness involves both righteousness and mercy, so repentance is the inner and full realization that we have violated not simply the law of God (that is, his righteousness) but also the love of God (that is, his very being as the Father). But this recognition that our sin consists essentially in a violation of God's love, while it means the immeasurable deepening of the significance of sin, means also the beginning of forgiveness. The Gospels sometimes add faith to repentance; but they do not need to, for repentance involves faith as a part of itself. We may be regretful or remorseful or despairing otherwise, but we cannot be *penitent* if we do not see our sin in the light of God's forgiveness. Indeed, a true realization of the fact and nature of our sin involves in itself a partial acceptance of forgiveness; that is, we cannot repent if we are not already in process of being forgiven. Repenting and being forgiven are two sides of a single act of realization, in which love and truth, righteousness and mercy, are inseparably fused.

This single act has unquestionably taken place within Paul's experience. He knows the reality of repentance and forgiveness. But his *interpretation* of this reality, his *explanation* of how it happens that within the new community of Christ he finds himself at peace with God—this explanation denies, in effect, the organic unity of the experience and, implicitly (although it was Marcion a generation or more later who was to draw the inference), the unity of God himself. For that interpretation obscures the fact that love has its own way of dealing with sin—a way that is compatible with the highest demands of truth, but that does not need to make use of the terms or devices of either the law court or the market place. We do not have to be acquitted before the Judge in order to be reconciled to the Father. The Father, as such, *forgives;* and all he asks is what a true father must always ask—penitence and trust. Forgiveness on God's part and penitence and trust on ours are the very atmosphere of the community that God brought into existence through the life, death and resurrection of Christ, and in which all the meaning of salvation is to be found. It is strange that Paul should know this so well and should be so eager to say it, and yet make so little use of the terms in which Jesus said it with such perfect adequacy and truth.

The Master knew that the best analogy furnished by our natural human life to the relationship in which we truly and ultimately stand to God and, therefore, to one another is that of the family. Paul, who without ever having listened to his words was yet his greatest disciple, is wanting to say just what Jesus was constantly saying—that any peace with God we can have must consist not in the awareness of being deserving, but in the assurance of being forgiven; not in the consciousness of being good enough to be loved, but in the knowledge that Another is good enough to love us. But in his actual saying of this, can we deny that Paul is hampered by his lack of insight into the appropriateness and truth of the family analogy, which Jesus intuitively seized on and constantly employed? It would be inviting the merest speculation to inquire just what, if anything, in Paul's early experience accounts for his making such slight use of the home as a type of kingdom of God. But, whatever the cause, there can be no doubt that in neglecting it he failed to see and use that part of our natural life that, at its best and most authentic, comes nearest to representing the ultimate, and therefore the essential and real, character of our existance.

We are concerned in these chapters rather with the religious experience of Paul than with his thought as such, but we can scarcely avoid noting two effects upon his theology of this neglect—effects that appear most clearly in the more doctrinal letters to the Galatians and the Romans. One of these effects has already been mentioned more than once in the last few pages: Paul is led to interpret the *death* of Christ as being a vicarious act of expiation, a satisfaction, in some sense, of God's righteous demands. Once God's action is conceived of as an "acquitting," a "declaring 'not guilty,' " a "treating as righteous," in a word, a "justification," the conception of Christ as performing a vicarious expiatory act becomes inevitable. Only such an act can explain how it is possible for God, who is perfectly righteous, to acquit sinners. A just judge may acquit if the demands of justice have been satisfied, but he cannot *forgive,* and any amount of penitence on a culprit's part is quite irrelevant in a courtroom. Details in Paul's view of how the death of Christ functioned to make acquittal possible are disputed by students of his letters, but surely it is clear that he regarded the death of Christ as having this effect.

The issue here needs to be carefully defined. There can be no possible question as to the central place of Christ's death in the Christian view of Christ. Not only was the crucifixion of Jesus in actual fact the very crux of the original divine event, in which God acted to save us and through which the new community was created, but also the cross perfectly represents the meaning of that act—its motive, its occasion, and its cost. It speaks with mighty power of the love of God, which in Christ did not stop short of complete identification with finite human beings, going so far as to suffer death, even such a death as this; and also, not less powerfully, of the desperate moral need of human beings, so blind and so possessed of evil as to be willing to nail him there. The cross thus signifies as nothing else could possibly do the awful seriousness of our sin, and therefore the depth and quality of the penitence that is required of us and that only the remembrance of it and the appropriation of its meaning can create in us. The supremacy of the cross in Christianity does not depend upon any particular explanation of it; that supremacy is essential and inalienable. But some explanations—of what does not need to be, and cannot be, explained—are less inadequate that others; and the explanation that on the cross of Christ the demands of God's justice were satisfied so that his mercy could legitimately be extended to sinners is surely not among the more adequate. It implies, as we have seen, divisions within the meaning of forgiveness and within the nature of God himself that are in the last resort intolerable. No one is likely to maintain that Paul held this view in any crass or consistent form—certainly that is not meant here—but can it be denied that his writings give some basis for it?

The second effect of Paul's neglect of the ideas of repentance and forgiveness is that it deprived him of the only possible theoretical ground for affirming the reality of ethical obligation within the Christian life. It is clear that for Paul, before his conversion, the only hope of peace with God lay in obedience to God's commandments as they were known in the Jewish law. The seventh chapter of the Epistle to the Romans tells of his struggles to give the required obedience and of his failure. He found (and I think he means to say that he still finds) a "law of sin" within his personality "at war with the law of [his] mind and making [him] captive to the law of sin which dwells in [his] members"; and the end of this struggle is the cry, "Wretched man that I am! Who will deliver me from this body of death?" It is often argued that this kind of experience was not the normal Jewish experience with the Torah (or "law"). Certainly it was not characteristic of *average* Judaism in the first century, any more than the strikingly similar experience of John Wesley was characteristic of Anglicanism in the eighteenth; but that does not mean that it was abnormal. It is the way in which a certain kind of morally serious religious person has time and again responded to the law of God; indeed, how else is such a person to respond if his or her response is to the *law* of God alone? Out of the despair to which this way inevitably led, Paul is brought into the community of love in which the contrite sinner finds himself forgiven of God—only, as we have seen, Paul does not *say* it so, preferring to speak of God as *justifying* the ungodly, and justifying him or her, not on the ground of repentance (what can repentance have to do with justification?), but on the ground of Christ's expiatory act, which one appropriates by faith. Thus we have a justification "apart from law" altogether (Rom. 3:21), and Paul's opponents might well ask, "Why then not sin that grace may abound? What ground is there for ethical obligation, once one is in Christ?"

Paul nowhere convincingly answers this question, and his raising it several times seems to show that he was troubled by it. His answer—most fully set forth in Rom. 6—takes the form of a demonstration that the believer *will* be righteous, not of an explanation of why he or she *ought* to be: since believers are in Christ, they will fulfill the law of Christ; since they have the Spirit, they will manifest the fruits of the Spirit. In the practical sections of his letters, to be sure, Paul shows himself not only aware that Christians actually often did not observe the law of Christ, but also ready urgently to insist that they are obligated to do so. But Paul has no persuasive *theoretical* basis for this insistence. Only by giving full place to the idea of the continuing necessity of repentance can one affirm the entire and only sufficiency of grace without destroying in theory the continuing validity of law. The answer to the question of the antinomians would seem to be that God's forgiveness is available only to the penitent, and repentance involves constant awareness of, and submission to, the righteous will of God. Would not this have been Jesus' answer—if indeed he would ever have laid himself open to such a question? Must we not acknowledge that Paul's neglect of this concept deprives him of a convincing theoretical ground for his insistence upon the *obligation* (as distinguished from the structural necessity) of ethical living for the Christian, as well as having the effect of setting law and grace in a wholly antithetical relation that has had fateful consequences in the history of the church?

The differences between Jesus and Paul may easily be exaggerated. As we conclude this part of our discussion, it is important that we remember what has been said several times, that the substance of forgiveness and repentance is at the very heart of Paul's gospel, despite his neglect of the concepts themselves. It was Jesus who told the parable of the prodigal son, and we can scarcely imagine it on the lips of Paul; but that story sets forth realities of grace that Paul had deeply experienced, and that he was constantly seeking to express. In and through the whole redemptive event—the life, teaching, death and resurrection of Christ—God was acting to *reconcile* the world to himself, and this reconciling act was his adopting and embracing us as his children. "When we cry, 'Abba! Father!' it is the Spirit himself bearing witness with our spirit that we are children of God, and if children, then heirs, heirs of God and fellow heirs with Christ" (Rom. 8:15-17).[2]

III

The forgiveness of God, as Paul received and interpreted it, brought with it a new moral freedom and power. This is the second aspect of the new life to which reference was made at the beginning of this chapter.

This second aspect corresponds to a second aspect of the human situation apart from Christ. We have seen that Paul knows himself, as a natural man, to be a sinner—that is, a transgressor of God's command, morally responsible for his acts and deserving the judgment of death because of them. As such he needs forgiveness, or justification and reconciliation. But he also knows himself to be the "slave of sin," a helpless victim, incapable of freeing himself from a bondage he hates, and which he knows ends inevitably in death. Paul's great autobiographical statement in Rom. 7:7-25 has been cited as a confession of guilt that he had no way of expiating; that passage is even more pertinent, however, in the present connection—as an acknowledgment of a slavery from which he could find no way of escape. The law is "spiritual," but he is "carnal, sold under sin." He does not understand his own actions, for he finds himself doing the very thing he hates. He even goes so far as to say, "It is no longer I that do it, but sin which dwells within me." And yet in other passages Paul expresses just as forcefully his awareness that it *is* he who "does it," and that he deserves death on account of it

This understanding of the nature of sin as being both transgression for which we are responsible and a slavery of which we are the helpless vic-

---

[2]For other views on this same problem discussed much too summarily in the foregoing pages, see expecially Vincent Taylor, *Forgiveness and Reconciliation* 2nd ed. (London: Macmillan, 1948). Taylor argues that the word *forgiveness* in Jesus' teaching means simply the remission of sins. But surely the idea of renewed fellowship is implicit. In any case, however, I have been concerned in this section primarily with ideas, not with words. After all, the word *forgiveness* is not found in Luke 15:11-32, and the word *justify* is found in Luke 18:9-14. Similarly, the word *repent* is found in neither of these passages, but the idea of repentance is at the heart of both. It is these ideas that do not appear, or appear differently, in Paul. See also two extended critical discussions of the views defended in this section, written, respectively, by Paul Schubert and C. F. D. Moule, in *Christian History and Interpretation* (Cambridge: University Press, 1967) 363-406.

tims may not be logically consistent, but it answers to the realities of the human situation. Any way of dealing with sin that presupposes that it is simply the one thing *or* the other is unrealistic—whether it is the characteristic way of the moralist, who holds that one has only to repent and to make a stronger effort, or of the determinist (whether psychiatrist, novelist, philosopher, or theologian), who denies both responsibility and guilt and, if he or she contemplates the possibility of salvation at all (as, of course, the psychiatrist and the theologian do), conceives of it entirely in terms of release from bondage. If we must make a choice betwen the two, let it be the second; but actually neither alternative is adequate. We know ourselves to be guilty, and we know ourselves to be helpless to do the perfect will of God. This is the nature of sin as it makes itself known in our experience. "Justification and reconciliation" is God's answer to our guilt; "redemption" is his answer to our bondage.

This redemption or deliverance (as indeed the reconciliation also) is an aspect of life within the kingdom of God; it is therefore essentially eschatological and cannot be fully received in this life. But, as we have also seen, a real foretaste of the life of the world to come has been given us in the Spirit, and thus we have actually received an advance installment of our inheritance of freedom and power. New moral resources are available to those who are made members of the body of Christ. Although sin has not yet been destroyed, it has been placed under sentence of death (Rom. 8:3), and our powers of resistance have been renewed and strengthened. Not only are believers forgiven, they are also given a new righteousness. This righteousness is not their own. They can claim no credit for it; indeed, they will not know it as righteousness at all. They will be aware only of God's goodness *toward* them, not of the working of that goodness *in* and *through* them. But others will see it, will thank God, and will take courage.

Whatever difficulties we may have with Paul's view that the believer is no longer under the law, we are bound to recognize the truth of his insight that whatever of true righteousness it is given us to have results, not from our obedience to law, but from God's gift of the Spirit. We were noting in the preceding chapter the fact that *living* things are always the work of God. This is true also of righteousness. There are two kinds of goodness—the goodness of the law and the goodness of the Spirit. The only goodness *we* can make is of the first kind. We make it by adding obedience to obedience, as a mason places bricks end to end and one on top of another. Such is legal goodness, and it is just as much alive as is a brick wall.

Such goodness, like a brick wall, is not without its important uses; it may well serve to protect one from certain evils to which the undisciplined person may succumb. But such goodness is sterile and, therefore, in the final reckoning spurious. True goodness is living and fruitful, and human beings cannot make it, no matter how hard they try. In fact, one's tense effort may get in the way of God's creative activity, as such effort often keeps an artist from producing his or her best work—and for the same reason. True goodness is God's goodness, not our own; it is God's gift, not our achievement. It is "God's love . . . poured into our hearts through the Holy Spirit which has been given to us." Or, to say the same thing only a little differently, it is participation in the new community of *agape,* which God miraculously brought into being in and through Christ Jesus our Lord.

And so we return at the end to the topic with which our discussion of Paul's religious life began. To be "in Christ" is to be a member of the ultimate, eschatological order, the divine community of love, proleptically present and partially realized in the church, whose spirit is the very Spirit of God and the very presence of the risen Christ. The Christian life is, essentially and definitively, life within that community. Within it, even now, are to be found forgiveness, peace with God, the joy of fellowship with Christ, and that beginning of victory over sin and fear and death which is the ground of a sure hope that we shall be "more than conquerors through him who loved us," and that "neither death, nor life, nor angels, nor principalities, nor things present, nor things to come, nor powers, nor height, nor depth, nor anything else in all creation, will be able to separate us from the love of God in Christ Jesus our Lord" (Rom. 8:37-39).

IV

We are thus reminded again that Paul thought of himself as being "a man in Christ" only in the sense in which other believers were also in Christ, the very word *Christ* in this context designating a shared, corporate life, a *koinonia.* We, however, are likely to think of this phrase, which he was apparently the first to use, as applying to Paul himself with particular aptness and force. We are likely to think of him as being in a real sense *the* "man in Christ." No one else of whom we have any record has manifested a devotion to Christ so utter and so strenuous, has come so near to being, in very truth, "Christ's slave," his whole life not only dominated but bounded by his love of Christ; and no one else has interpreted the meaning of Christ so profoundly, so truly, so creatively. The "meaning of Christ" means more, of course, than the conscious intention of Jesus' teachings—although, despite the differences that have been noted in this chapter, Paul understood the intention, so far as we can know, better than any of Jesus' own disciples. But the "meaning of Christ" goes beyond this, involving a reference not simply to Jesus but to the whole event, including his person and teaching, his death and resurrection, through which God acted to bring the New Israel into being. Although no interpretation of that event that is not consonant with Jesus' teaching could be true, nevertheless it was impossible that the event should have been fully interpreted in the teaching—impossible both because the teaching was itself a part of the event and because the event had not fully transpired when the teaching was given. Paul became the first great interpreter of the complete event, as he became the first great apostle of Christ among the nations. In him was first fulfilled in a conspicuous way the word of Christ: "Greater works than these will he do, because I go to the Father."

As apostle he carried the gospel across half the ancient world and, almost single-handed, laid the foundations of Gentile Christianity; as interpreter he set the lines Christian theology was to follow, through Mark, to John, and beyond; and at many points he spoke himself what has proved to be the final word. The marks of human frailty can be discerned in his work, but to the really discerning they serve only to make more clear the supreme greatness of his achievement—or rather the supreme greatness of what God wrought through him.

Index of Scripture Passages

Index of Names and Subjects